MW00791836

Ten lessons in love

Ten lessons in love

Miles Olsen

Copyright © Miles Olsen 2023

All rights reserved. No part of this book may be reproduced or
used in any manner without written permission of the copyright
owner except for the use of quotations in a book review.

The events and conversations in this book have been set down to
the best of the author's ability, although some names and details
have been changed to protect the privacy of individuals.

Cover photograph via istock
First paperback edition June 2023

ISBN 978-1-7774652-3-0 (paperback)

milesolsen.com

One

A week before Kevin died, we had a conversation I will never forget. He had been in a bleak place for months leading up to this moment, and after years of struggle and isolation, something in him seemed to have broken.

"When I get through this, Miles," he said, "I need to change my life. I need people. I'm too alone, and it's killing me. I'm not sure how to go about it, but I've removed myself from humanity for too long. It's been a mistake - a huge mistake. I took my isolation too far, and I regret it."

His words had a heaviness and remorse that were uncharacteristic of him. Something had happened that humbled his usually unapologetic, defiant personality. His fragility as a lone man had become terrifyingly clear - he realized he needed something more than himself. He realized that without connection, without actively stepping into the river of humanity, he was a tree torn out of the earth, uprooted and cut off from his source of life.

"I don't know how to go about it," he continued. "Maybe I have to get a random job that connects me to lots of people? I have no idea what to do, and it honestly terrifies me. But something absolutely must change. Please, do not let me forget this."

But before that change could happen, Kevin was gone. He chose to end his story and took his life before the next chapter could begin.

In the aftermath of his death, my world felt like a bomb had gone off in it. I stumbled in shock and confusion through the wasteland left in the wake of an enormous loss. I felt crushed by a world of grief, pounded by waves of confusion, guilt, and sadness that I could not anticipate, reason with, or ignore. It was like reality broke, the heartbeat of life skipped, and someone fundamental was gone. Nothing about it made sense, and all I knew to do was take time to feel everything, talk with a friend on the phone when I could, read books, and go for walks. It felt like life would never be okay again - the grief seemed like it would go on forever.

In this state, I had no interest in the trivial pleasures or worries that usually occupied my attention. Things like love, sex, and worldly accomplishments felt pointless - social acceptance and the fear of judgment seemed disgustingly unimportant. The idea of giving such things any amount of mental space was absurd. *We all die - who cares?*

I felt an apathy, almost a nihilism, that was somehow liberating. I realized that most of what I typically worried about and focused on throughout daily life was meaningless. Losing someone in such a tragic, sudden way shook me awake to what mattered. And it was sobering to acknowledge that almost nothing I normally gave power or attention to in life mattered.

Over time, the waves of grief began to mellow. The space between them started to stretch out longer and longer. And in those spaces, in those moments of calm, I began to look up at the wreckage of my life. During one of these moments, I remembered that conversation with Kevin. I remembered the regret he shared with me about his loneliness and the urgency in his voice.

He had chosen a path of chronic, self-imposed isolation that, in the end, he called a mistake. As I surveyed the isolation and emptiness of my own life at that moment, I knew I had made the same mistake as him.

For years, I embarked on a path that mirrored Kevin's in many ways. I pulled away from my family, friendships, romantic relationships, and career to focus on emotional work, introspection, and a kind of inner healing with reckless abandon. I had felt emboldened, encouraged, and supported by Kevin's friendship and presence. He was always a few steps further than me - he was the comrade cheering me along.

Gradually, I followed my friend's footsteps into a desert. I walked away from nearly all participation in the river of humanity. It was a lonely path, and it was uncomfortable. But there was always an assumption that the desert would transform once we healed enough of our trauma - once we had done the inner work. A new, pure life would blossom. Like-minded people would arrive. Something completely different would take shape. But it never did.

Things seemed to get only more bleak and empty as the years passed. I devoted more time and energy to emotional work. I stepped further away from people. And while something beautiful grew in me, my world became increasingly lonely and empty. I purified my life to the point of desolation. I stepped away from imperfect connections until almost nothing was left, except for Kevin. And then he was gone.

Now I was alone, and the isolation he described as a tragic error was something I had to face - a mistake I was still living. I had been on what I thought was a path of healing, yet this is where I ended up: My life was in shambles. I was broke, confused, and mourning the suicide of my closest friend. The more I tried to fix myself, the more my world seemed to disintegrate.

In the period that followed Kevin's death, these were some of the reflections, questions, and conversations that poured through me. I didn't know what to think or do, but the moment I found myself in was sobering. I was lost and alone, and it was dawning on me that I, too, needed something much more than myself.

Two

Several months after Kevin passed away, I ran into my old friend, Pandora. We crossed paths when I was walking along the ocean on a sunny spring afternoon. It had been years since we last saw each other or spoke, and there was a mutual sense of excitement and curiosity as we said hello.

After exchanging a hug, we sat on a bench by the water and took turns sharing updates about our lives. I described everything happening in my world, including the grief and isolation I was living through.

Something was immediately comfortable and easy about talking with Pandora. There was an awkwardness and distance between us due to the years that had passed since we last spoke, but I also felt the warmth of an old, trusted friend. And, at that moment, I desperately needed a friend.

During a break in our conversation, Pandora looked into my eyes and said: "Miles, I've been worried about you for a while. The last time I saw you was maybe two or three years ago? You looked so run down. It was like your spark was gone - you felt like a withering, wilted plant. The joyful, inspired person I used to know wasn't there anymore. You seemed so deflated, so unhappy. It was hard for me to witness."

I wanted to understand what Pandora was talking about, so I asked her to explain what she had seen in more detail.

"I'm not sure the best way to describe it," she continued, "but it looked like you were dying inside. The Miles I knew as a boisterous, fun, passionate person had shrivelled up. You stopped believing in yourself - you stopped letting yourself just *be*. It was like your light was going out, and it was getting worse each time I saw you."

I couldn't quite wrap my head around what Pandora was saying - but it was something she would repeat many times as we rekindled our friendship over the coming months: She had been concerned for me (and I got the sense that she still was).

After that initial encounter, Pandora and I began to meet for walks along the water regularly. There was a lot of catching up to do, as many things had happened in the years since we'd last been close.

One afternoon, we sat on top of a driftwood log on the beach as I described my recent experiences with dating and women. Something I said sparked a thought in Pandora, and she interrupted my story with a sudden idea: She wanted me to meet someone - an acquaintance that she was convinced I would get along with.

"There's something about you two that seems like it would just click," she explained. "You have got to meet her - you two could be good friends!"

She reached for her phone and searched for a picture to show me.

"Here," she said, handing me her phone with a poorly lit photo of a young woman on its screen.

"That's Maya. It's not the best photo, but it gives you an idea of what she looks like - it gives you a sense of her vibe." As Pandora spoke, she looked intently at my face to study my reaction.

Maya was beautiful, and as much as I could tell from a photo, she looked like a sensitive, introverted, deep person. I didn't understand why Pandora was so excited about connecting the two of us. Still, when she asked if it was okay to pass my phone number along to Maya, I had no hesitation before saying yes. I had been saying no to life for so long that it felt like I had to start saying yes to something.

"I'm not suggesting you two should date or anything," Pandora added. "She is quite a bit younger than you and at a very different place in her life. But I think you two should meet. She needs friends as much as you do, and there's something that I think you two have in common."

About a week after that conversation on the beach, Maya called me out of the blue. I was surprised to hear from her and wide open to talking. After an awkward start to the conversation, we ended up speaking for a couple of hours. We chatted about our lives, loves, challenges, and dreams. I remember very little of the conversation except for a glowing warmth in my chest that started about thirty minutes in and grew stronger and warmer as we continued talking. By the end of our conversation, the feeling in my chest was almost ecstatic.

I also remember Maya saying that our chat was not normal for her, that we spoke with a kind of openness and honesty she felt she needed more than anything. But she also said that it terrified her.

The conversation ended with us excited to get to know one another better. I encouraged Maya to reach out whenever she wanted to chat again or meet up in real life, and we said goodbye.

As I got off the phone, the glowing, warm feeling in my chest became almost overwhelming, and I decided to lie down on the floor of my apartment to bask in it. I wondered if this blissful sensation was a symptom of my becoming infatuated with Maya or if it was just what it felt like to talk openly with a kindred spirit. It didn't matter - I didn't need to understand it - it felt like heaven.

That evening, I sent Maya a message thanking her for the conversation and repeating my invitation to talk or hang out any time. It felt right to leave it in her hands to decide when we would connect next (and to let her know that I was wide open).

A month passed after that conversation, and Maya didn't respond. Now and again, Pandora would ask if Maya had gotten back to me, and the answer was always the same: Not yet. After a while, we both assumed I would never hear back from her. This, it turned out, was its own kind of medicine.

I got very excited about meeting Maya in the days and weeks after that call with her. The volcanic eruption I felt in my heart when we spoke was like a miraculous sign of life in a desert. After so long alone, feeling that connection with someone, even if only through a phone call and for a few minutes, sparked my hope, curiosity, and desire. It felt like a missing element had reappeared in my world - a light I had been living without returned in the form of Maya. I could barely contain my excitement.

But at the same time, there was a strange panic in me: This beauty had shown itself, and now part of me was ready to cling to it for dear life. I hadn't even met Maya yet, but that conversation with her had awakened a hunger in me, and I desperately wanted to feel more.

As the weeks passed, the glowing sensation in my heart slowly faded. The jittery excitement in me had nowhere to go. I cycled through feelings of confusion, frustration, and resentment toward Maya. I wrote several messages to send her, eager to connect - but something stopped me every time I was about to hit send. It was like an invisible hand grabbed and held me back, ensuring I stayed alone in my discomfort.

Gradually, I recognized what was happening: The possibility of sharing love with a woman had brushed past me, and a wild, panicked desire for that love had been stirred. I couldn't help but wonder if Maya, a sensitive, empathic woman, could somehow feel the intensity of my longing - and was being pushed away by it. Having a stranger heap so much hope and desperation at you could feel suffocating.

Without any word from Maya, I was left alone to sit with this hungry void in me. Instead of laying on my apartment floor with an ecstatic warmth in my chest or spending time with the woman I had become fixated on, I went for long walks with a feeling of loneliness and restlessness swirling in me.

I suspected that this was the gift Maya had come into my world to deliver: A sobering reminder of how easily I could fall apart in the presence of a woman. My weakness had been revealed.

Once I acknowledged all of this, it didn't take long for the pained yearning that had been awakened in me to start calming down. I remembered that Maya was just a person, and I had been happy and complete before her brief appearance in my world. It had been exciting to feel a momentary glimpse of connection with her, but that's all it was. I had to let go of my expectations and desire for something more. I reminded myself that I didn't know Maya at all. And, as the days passed, I started to let it go.

Then, one sunny afternoon, she called. I had given up on hearing from her entirely, so I was surprised by the sound of her voice.

As we spoke, Maya shared that she had been struggling with severe depression and anxiety over the past month. She apologized for not reaching out sooner and explained that it had been due to her feeling so low.

I shared what I had gone through since we last spoke, with a sense of humour and detachment around my passionate emotions, having already emerged from my storm of anxious attachment. I wondered out loud if I needed to get some of my feelings settled before we could have a grounded conversation - if my intensity would have scared Maya away. She confirmed this was probably the case - she might have run from so much emotion and excitement pouring out of a man she didn't know. After a brief chat, Maya asked me if I would like to meet up in person that night, which I was wide open to.

It was a warm June evening when we met in Maya's neighbourhood for a walk. As I got to the busy intersection we had chosen as a meeting place, I recognized Maya from across the street. She was wearing a baggy, oversized jean jacket that was unbuttoned with a very revealing, tiny crop top underneath. I found that a fascinating combination - her outfit simultaneously hid her body and was highly revealing.

Even from across the street, there was an intensity to Maya that was apparent. She seemed uncomfortable, nervous, and maybe caught up in anxious thoughts. She was also physically beautiful, though I had promised myself I wouldn't get carried away idolizing her feminine beauty immediately.

Once we said hello and made our way to a quiet side street, Maya didn't take long to open up. It was almost instant.

Our conversation flowed like a stream as I asked questions and listened to her with wide-eyed curiosity. Maya explained that she hadn't been doing very well and, like me, lacked human connection. She shared some of the struggles she had been facing and the trauma she was coming to terms with. I found myself nodding along, understanding and empathizing with her challenges.

After walking and speaking for a while, Maya paused, looked at me, and said: "I can't believe I just felt comfortable sharing all of that with you. I feel like I could trust you with my life now!"

There was a mutual appreciation and comfort between us, an easy, quick, deep understanding we shared despite having lived very different lives.

As the sun set, we sat in a grassy park bordered by busy city streets and continued to talk. We spoke about relationships, and Maya shared her cynicism around men, sex, and the possibility of ever experiencing a genuine intimate connection. By this time, it had gotten dark, and we stared at the star-filled sky above us as we spoke.

After venting about the hopelessness of love, men, and romance, Maya changed her tone momentarily and said: "I don't know. Maybe I am ready for a relationship, and maybe there *is* something beautiful that I'm ready to experience."

Just as she finished sharing that thought, a shooting star streamed across the night sky.

"Did you see that?" I asked her.

"See what?" she responded.

Maya hadn't noticed the shooting star and seemed perplexed by my excitement. I was nearly jumping up and down, convinced that this was a sign of some kind.

I wondered if it was a heavenly confirmation of what Maya had just been saying - a confirmation that she was ready for love. Although, in retrospect, maybe it was telling that she hadn't seen the light herself - only I had.

Eventually, the grass in the park became cold and wet with late-night dew, and I walked Maya back to her house. When we got to her front door, she asked me if I wanted to come inside and hang out in her bedroom for a while. A part of me was instantly nervous and excited at this - the likelihood that things were about to get physical seemed very high. I did my best to contain myself and calmly said yes.

Maya's place was a shabby, dilapidated old home shared with a handful of young roommates. Her bedroom was tiny - nothing more than a walk-in closet outfitted with a single mattress on the floor, a side table, and a dresser. It was dimly lit, carefully decorated, and had a surprisingly comforting atmosphere.

As I stood and looked around, Maya sat on her bed and invited me to join her. I awkwardly sat down on the edge of the mattress, feeling tense and unnatural. I had no idea what to do or how to act in this situation. Because Maya was a completely new person (and nearly ten years younger than me), I felt stilted and uncomfortable. She laid down on the bed and asked if I wanted to cuddle. I did.

Once I lay beside her, she grabbed my body and pulled it up against hers, wrapping one of my arms around her waist. As we cuddled, Maya's voice changed in a way that confused me: It became more high-pitched, submissive, and younger sounding. Even the way she spoke - her cadence and choice of words - seemed completely different. It sounded more like a child's voice than the complex, intelligent woman I had been talking to all night.

If we hadn't spoken so openly and honestly up to that point, I might not have noticed this shift or been bothered by it. But as things were, it felt like the person I had been connecting with in such a sincere and open way had left. It felt like a different Maya was here now, and she was playing a role or game. There was a disconnect - a distance between us that was jarring. Eventually, this became so perplexing that I had to say something. We'd been having a conversation all night centred around honesty, so I honestly named what I felt - as gently and kindly as I knew how to.

Maya immediately acknowledged everything I described, seeming to snap out of a trance as she responded. She agreed that something had changed when we got to her room - she felt herself regress into an old pattern that she had with men, falling into the role of a submissive girl. She shared that it didn't feel good, but it wasn't something she understood well or had control over. I didn't pretend to understand it, either. I just wanted to be honest, and we both agreed that talking about it did feel better than not saying anything.

None of this took away from how good it felt to lie there with Maya. And for a long time, we rested in her bed, our bodies pressed together in silence.

After nearly falling asleep beside her, I left Maya's place and biked home in the warm summer night. As I coasted down empty streets, I felt exhausted, excited, and messed up inside - I felt more alive than I had in a long time.

The following morning, I woke up to a message from Maya asking what I was doing that night. I had no plans, and we decided to get together again. This time, Maya came to my neighbourhood.

When she arrived at my apartment that evening, she was visibly shaken. The busyness, chaos, and commotion of passing through downtown en route to my place seemed to have triggered her anxiety, so I welcomed her into my little apartment and, unsure of what to do or what was happening, suggested we relax for a bit.

Maya could barely speak, she was so agitated, and I was somewhat confused by her state. After sitting in my little apartment for a couple of hours, she slowly began to calm down and relax. By the time it was getting dark outside and the busyness of daytime activity had faded, we decided to go for a walk.

For the rest of the evening, we walked through my neighbourhood's parks and side streets and talked. I could feel how Maya's anxiety distanced us - at moments bringing a halt to conversation altogether. And yet there was something magnetic, beautiful, and disarming about her rawness and sensitivity.

It was late when we eventually got back to my place, and Maya asked if it was okay for her to stay the night. There was no hesitation in me - she was more than welcome.

At this point, I wasn't sure what was going on between us. I was attracted to Maya, but she was in so much mental anguish that we weren't flirting or building a sense of chemistry. I had no intention of making a move on her, but I was moved by her beauty and personality.

Once we got into bed, Maya's restlessness seemed to calm down almost instantly. Something about our bodies coming together felt more straightforward and peaceful than any of the talking we'd been engaging in up to that point - it just fit. Where our minds had been struggling to connect and understand each other, now our bodies could communicate more simply and directly. It felt grounding, nourishing, and natural. We lay in each other's arms for a long time before falling asleep.

That night marked the beginning of my romantic relationship with Maya. We had only just met and quickly moved from strangers to lovers. I could tell that our connection wasn't something casual. An instant emotional bond formed between us, and I felt comfortable with that. There had been times in the past when I could feel this type of bond begin to form with a woman, and it made me want to run. That was not the case with Maya. There was something about being with her that felt good.

As we began talking every day and spending more time together, I could see things others might have considered red flags: Maya's crippling struggle with anxiety and depression, our age difference, etc. But none of that mattered to me. I sensed I was walking onto unstable ground with Maya, but I had been saying no to life and love for too long. For once, I had to say yes. Maya had an open heart and was open to me. We talked about our feelings and shared an emotional, soulful connection I had forgotten was possible. I quickly realized that the depth and sensitivity which caused Maya so much anguish in life also probably made it possible for her to connect in an unbelievably beautiful way. Given all of this, none of those red flags mattered. Not for the time being, at least.

After seeing each other for a few months, Maya confessed something to me: She had a part-time job working at a cafe, and it was a daily occurrence for men to come into her workplace and flirt with her. She had gotten into the habit of flirting back with some of these men. It was fun, made work more interesting, and it felt exhilarating to exchange playful words and sexual energy with men who were attracted to her.

Now that she was dating me, Maya explained how she found herself conflicted by these previously innocuous interactions. Earlier that day, she had a particularly flirtatious, sexually charged exchange with a man that caused her a crisis of conscience. She came home after work and impulsively shared everything with me.

"I don't want to be with anyone other than you, Miles," she explained, "but this kind of flirting is a habit that I don't know how to turn off. Honestly, it feels good getting that kind of attention from men. But afterwards, when I remember you, I feel horrible. I feel like I'm a horrible person and don't deserve to have you in my life."

It amazed me that, without provocation, Maya had shared this with me from the bottom of her heart and apologized with sincerity and compassion. I was blown away by her honesty.

Maya acknowledged that she wasn't sure how to stop herself from flirting with men in the future: "I just have a pattern of interacting with men in a certain way," she admitted. "It's something I have done my whole life - seeking attention and validation from men. I want to change, but I don't know how."

Sitting and listening, I didn't feel jealous, which almost confused me. Maya was confessing to flirting and feeding flames of attraction and sexual chemistry with lots of handsome men regularly. And yet her spontaneous act of honesty was so profound - such a soothing and reassuring gesture - that I felt I could trust her more, not less. It surprised me, but I didn't care about her flirting or feeding off the attention of other men - if she respected me enough to tell me about it. The honesty destroyed what would have otherwise been triggering: Secrets. If it was all out in the open, I somehow felt fine.

In a way, this budding relationship was an experiment in honesty for both of us. We tried to talk about everything and develop a common language of love and emotion. We learned what it felt like when one of us had become closed or distant and what it felt like when we were open. When we felt disconnected or like one of us was keeping a secret, we talked about it (to the best of our limited ability). After so many years without a woman in my life, without exchanging physical touch, and without the nourishment of emotional connection, Maya's arrival in my world felt like a godsend.

As time passed, Maya noticed something was keeping me from fully sinking into being with her. She felt that she was completely open to this relationship, but I was not. When she pointed out this disparity, I realized she was correct. Part of me was on the fence, unable to sink into this connection or see it as something with a future, and at the heart of my hesitation appeared to be the very thing that drew me to Maya: Her hypersensitivity (and probably my own, too). She was wildly open and sensitive in a way that allowed us to connect incredibly deeply. There were no emotional protections, defences, or barriers to intimacy when she opened up. It was amazing. But this sensitive, hyper-empathic aspect of her personality could also shut down connection entirely. It often drew her deep into isolating spirals of anxiety, taking her far away into a distant place in herself. So as much as her sensitivity could lead to a raw and unhindered connection, it could completely shut it down at any moment.

The more I got to know Maya, the more I saw glimpses of where her inner struggles could have originated. I also became humbled by the magnitude of her suffering. I could relate to almost every detail of it - the self-loathing, discomfort with body image, debilitating fear of rejection, etc. But Maya's version of these struggles seemed far more intense than mine. The pain and trauma of her past seemed more complex and shattering, too. She felt like a magnified version of me in some ways: More open, loving, and sensitive. More hurt by this world. More capable of trusting and surrendering to life - and more vulnerable to feeling crushed by it or losing herself in its noise.

From the beginning of our time together, I slipped into the role of a caretaker. When Maya was racked with anxiety, I patiently tried to offer support and help, with mixed results. Often, I would end up doing a kind of emotional work with her that I had spent the past several years practicing on myself. If she was paralyzed by shame and anxiety, I might ask if she wanted some help. With her blessing, I would begin exploring what she was feeling as though I was studying my own emotions.

And sometimes, to my astonishment, Maya would relax. Maybe because she was such a sensitive person, Maya could be very receptive to my attempts at supporting and calming her.

But this had unintended consequences: It further entrenched my role as a caretaker in our relationship. And it appeared to foster a sense of disempowerment in Maya. To say this another way: My attempts to lift Maya out of her pain quickly backfired when she inevitably dropped back into it. Then, she would feel almost more lost than before. I had come along, meddled with her, and given the impression that someone else had an answer.

After a while, Maya started to feel guilty about this dynamic. She felt like a leech that was becoming dependent on my caretaking and didn't like that. On my end, I started becoming more easily frustrated and agitated by her.

But even when I felt frustrated or drained, there was a sense of appreciation for Maya. The struggles I could see playing out in her were not unlike mine. She had been living in an isolated desert of her own. Consequently, she had a gnawing hunger for attention, energy, and validation. I could relate.

Much of her suffering came from an insecurity and a lack of self-love. It led to an inexhaustible appetite for validation from the outside. But no amount of external reassurance seemed to pacify it for long. No amount of attention or energy from another seemed fill its sense of emptiness. I knew something about that, too.

Like Maya, a part of me yearned for external validation. This part wanted to feel better about itself, even if only for a second. And for this part of me, the feeling of being relied upon - the feeling of being *needed* by Maya in her suffering - was one hell of a drug.

But regardless of how good it felt to be needed by her, it seemed that the more I extended my so-called help and support to Maya, the worse off she was. I would try to show her things I had learned about emotional work or meditation, then step back and watch her use these tools to fuel her anxiety and self-hatred in new and disturbing ways. My attempts at help often seemed like they further entrenched her sense of being flawed and fed into the idea that she was a problem to solve. The more I tried to fix her, the more I reinforced the idea that she needed to be fixed.

One day while I was visiting Maya, something caught me off guard. She had been in a bleak place for a while, reaching out for help and support more than usual. I felt checked out and numb - like I had stretched myself too thin for too long and was barely present while we spent the afternoon together. As she lay immobile in her bed, I sat beside her in an empty, distant state, and something spontaneously clicked in me: I knew we would break up. It was like I could see an end on the horizon, and it shocked me.

My heart sank, and my throat tightened into a painful lump. I didn't want what I was feeling to be true - I didn't want this to end. But as I rode my bike home that night, I had a sad, sober sense that if I wanted to be responsible and loving to either of us, we needed to stop what we were doing. In my gut, it felt like it was already over.

For the next couple of weeks, I couldn't shake this feeling. I talked with friends about it and tried to get a sense of objectivity or clarity. I wanted them to tell me I was crazy and just running from intimacy, but nobody did.

When I spoke to Pandora, her perspective was not what I wanted to hear: "You two don't really make sense together," she said. "Isn't that obvious? It doesn't seem like it would work - not even a bit."

My heart sank as she spoke.

"As friends, you two make sense," she continued. "But lovers? I think your gut is trying to tell you something so you can save yourself from more pain by dragging this thing out indefinitely. It's not going to work."

I wanted to disagree with Pandora and make a case for giving this relationship a fair chance - but despite my resistance, it was like my body had already made a choice. A part of me had already checked out and started to leave, but my mind couldn't comprehend why or how this was happening.

After much soul-searching and reflection, I decided to talk with Maya about what I was going through. I had no idea what my feelings meant, and I certainly wasn't interested in breaking up - but keeping such strong feelings hidden from her felt wrong.

So, in the spirit of transparency, I told Maya everything. It was awkward and painful, but I opened up about my entire process. When I finished explaining the confusing thoughts and feelings I'd been navigating, Maya responded straightforwardly: "So, you're breaking up with me? *Fuck*."

She spoke with a pained look as though she'd been kicked in the gut.

I began explaining that I was not breaking up with her - I was just sharing feelings I didn't understand. But Maya's reaction was so strong I could barely get a word in. She was blindsided, in shock and disbelief. And as I searched for the right words to explain that I was not ending things, it dawned on me that, given everything I just said, it almost certainly sounded like this conversation was a breakup. I sat in stunned silence at the mess I had created for a moment while Maya reeled in pain. Then, I made a split-second decision that took me by surprise. A voice in my head said: *Just go with this. You know it's inevitable. You've broken something here. Let it fall to pieces. Don't drag out the pain - let this be the end.*

At that moment, I decided I wouldn't argue with Maya or try to correct her any longer. Instead, I would go along with her interpretation of my words - I would let this be a breakup.

Two

Part of my rationale here was that the notion of having this torturous conversation repeatedly sounded awful. I didn't want to put her through that, so I would make this simple - Maya thought this was a breakup, and I would go along with that.

When I left Maya's house after that conversation, I couldn't believe what I'd just done. That was not supposed to have happened. But it did, and now there was no turning back.

As my doubts and regrets began settling in, another part of me answered them. It was a voice that believed I knew exactly what I was doing - that I had just made an honest, responsible, and courageous choice. It was very sure about this.

The following morning, I woke up to a handful of furious text messages from Maya. Together, they formed a passionate assault on my character, including accusations that I had been manipulative and hurtful. Just as I finished reading them, she called.

Maya was still angry and picked up where her messages left off, voicing her rage and declaring how poorly she thought of me.

Typically, my instinct would have been to defend myself and send some of Maya's anger back in her direction. But, given the circumstances, I had a different reaction. After she thoroughly vented, my only response was: "I think it might be good for you to be angry at me."

I knew that anger exists to create boundaries - it's the emotion that shows up when we need to protect ourselves and establish our safety or autonomy. And that's what Maya needed - to create a separation between herself and me. I had been allowed into the centre stage of her life, and I needed to be pushed out of that position now. She had to reorganize her emotional landscape, and getting pissed off at me would probably be a very effective way of accomplishing this.

So instead of trying to defend myself or coddle her, I finally stepped down from my caretaker position and respected her anger. I even encouraged it. My ego didn't like the idea of her being mad at me, but it had to take the hit.

She seemed to like this encouragement. And though it made her laugh and softened her rage somewhat, she was angry enough that it didn't fade away entirely.

Over the following days, Maya sent me text messages alternating between furious takedowns, heartfelt gratitude, and emergency calls for help while I restrained my indignation and caretaking. There was a squirming discomfort in me at letting this all be - in letting our two realities start to separate. It was excruciating.

As the weeks and months passed, those feelings mellowed, and I eventually found something remarkable on the other side of them: An ex-lover who slowly, over time, became a real friend.

Although my romantic relationship with Maya was brief and tumultuous, it felt like an infusion of love and intimacy into an otherwise sterile, desolate world. Maybe both of us were too sensitive and isolated from life to build a stable relationship - but that didn't matter to me. I had gotten to share love, and even if it was for just a moment, it felt like heaven after so much time alone.

I couldn't dwell for long on the fact that it didn't last or become something more, because I knew that neither of those things were true: Something in me had changed in a lasting way from my contact with Maya. I learned something new about love from her wide-open, effusive, unguarded heart. I didn't learn this from anything she said, and it was not something I could easily reduce to words myself. It was a soulful, pure, innocent, and vulnerable love. It was a gate flung fully open with no hesitation. I had received it from her, we had exchanged it, and now I knew how to feel it - I carried it in me.

Three

During the winter after my breakup with Maya, I had
the urge to reach out to my old friend, Mike Keelan. It
had been years since I last spoke to Mike or even
thought about him, but suddenly it was hard to get him
out of my head. In quiet moments, memories and
feelings of love for my old friend sprang out of
nowhere, so much so that it confused me. I couldn't stop
a flood of nostalgia and emotion around Mike. It felt as
though, after years of separation, he was somehow close
again.

Mike and I met years earlier and quickly formed a
special bond. I was in my mid-twenties at the time -
Mike was probably in his mid-fifties. He lived near my
backwoods home (a rugged, hand-built cabin I shared
with some close friends) and was introduced to me by a
mutual friend - my younger brother, Lenny - who
thought we might get along.

Mike was an unusually warm, curious, and engaging
man. When we first met, he sincerely invited me to
come by his place and visit him anytime. Drawn to his

openness and warmth, I accepted Mike's initial invitation and enjoyed spending time with him so much that I began to drop by his home regularly. It soon became one of the highlights of my days and weeks. Dropping by a friend's place to sit back and talk about life's suffering, joys, and mysteries with shared passion was a rare treasure.

Most of the time, I would drop by Mike's house unannounced, and if he was around (which he usually was), we would sit on the front porch of his humble, one-bedroom home and talk about life. Our conversations were often accompanied by cigarettes (which Mike constantly smoked), beer, or some of his homemade wine - and they stretched on for hours.

Mike's place was a social hub for an assortment of characters, so what would begin as an impromptu conversation between the two of us on his porch might evolve into a larger event as friends and acquaintances spontaneously dropped by and joined us.

It would not be unusual for me to stay at Mike's well into the evening and then have to make the trip back to my cabin in the dark with no flashlight - stumbling through the forest path home by memory and feeling, a bit tipsy from the beverages we drank and high from the conversation we shared.

There was a closeness and a warmth I experienced with Mike that I didn't quite understand at the time. When I left his place after a visit, he would often pause, look me in the eye, and say: "Miles, I love you."

The way he said those words was so direct and sincere that it felt like he knew something I didn't: He knew to never hold those words back.

We were two men at different places in our lives who came together to share our questions, challenges, desires, and wide-eyed philosophical curiosity. We talked about our love lives, about society, about difficult friendships - we talked about everything.

There was a realness and a brotherhood I experienced with Mike that was a blessing. I didn't comprehend just how unusual this was at the time - although I knew it was why an assortment of people were always stopping by his house: He was open to them, he was curious about them, and he made them feel welcomed - which might be one of the best feelings in the world.

The last time I saw Mike, I told him I had gotten rid of all my belongings and would be disappearing for a while. I explained that I didn't know how long I would be gone, but it would probably be years before we spoke again. His reaction was typical of his character.

"You're going on your hero's journey, Miles," he said with quiet enthusiasm. "It's something you have to do. I get it, brother. I'm gonna miss you, but I'm happy for you."

He gave me a firm handshake and a long, tight hug, and we said goodbye. Walking down his dusty driveway, I wondered if I might never see or speak to my friend Mike again.

It had been six years since that farewell, and now, for reasons I did not understand, Mike was constantly in my thoughts. Waves of gratitude and appreciation washed over me at seemingly random moments. Those years of separation gave me a deeper appreciation for Mike's role in my life - I now understood that he had shown me a kind of love and acceptance that was one of the greatest gifts possible.

In a way, the path of isolation I had embarked on since our farewell was the opposite of Mike's. Where I had pulled away from friends, family, and the world, Mike had lived as the open heart of a community. His cozy little home (a rustic, modified double-wide trailer) was a gathering place for a ragtag assortment of characters who called him their friend. Mike embraced all of them, finding the common thread between himself and the imperfect, sometimes challenging people who crossed his path. The messiness of humanity that I had turned away from was something Mike had chosen to be a beacon of unwavering openness to.

As weeks passed, and I continued to be consumed by these thoughts of gratitude, I wanted to reach out to Mike - to send him a message telling him how much he meant to me and how much I loved him. But a combination of insecurity and distraction pushed this urge to the side.

I wondered if Mike would still be open to me. After all, I had vanished from his world for many years - he might have developed some hard feelings toward me over that time. Because of my fears and hesitations, I postponed reaching out. Whenever I felt the urge to write him, I would find a reason to put it off.

But the feeling would not go away. It was there on my walks, in quiet moments alone, and even sometimes amid the busyness of work. I felt a sense of gratitude like a treasure chest glowing in me. And this was accompanied by an urge to share my appreciation with Mike - to let this man know I loved him. Still, I hesitated.

One day, I wondered if Mike was dead and if this was why I felt such an intense connection to him. I went online and searched for obituaries under his name and found nothing. Given the number of people who loved him, there surely would have been plentiful evidence of his passing if it had happened, so I was able to rule that out.

Then, one night, I had a dream about Mike. I was walking through a lush field with my brother, Lenny. Fruit and nut trees grew throughout this field, and we knew Mike had planted them there years ago. We stood and stared at these trees in awe. At the end of the dream, I wrote a letter to Mike, but it was not a letter I planned on sending to him - because I knew, as I was writing it, that Mike was dead.

When I woke up, before my mind could jump in and interpret what had just happened, I had a distinct feeling in my gut that Mike was gone. Minutes later, I turned on my phone and discovered a new message from Lenny (who, like Mike, I had not spoken to in six years). The message stated very plainly: "Mike Keelan died yesterday."

My head started spinning. I could not believe what I was reading, what I had just dreamed, or what I had been feeling (and ignoring) for the past month.

I spent that day in a stunned mix of emotions. There was a feeling of love for Mike. And there was sadness that I would never be able to talk to him again. I would never be able to drop by that hidden porch of his unannounced - to see him emerge from his doorway with an enormous smile plastered across his face, ready to hear my latest news and to share his. I would never be able to give him a copy of the book I planned on writing someday. I would never get to tell him how special he was and how much he meant to me.

The most bitter part of this was that I had my chance. For an entire month, my body had been screaming at me to send Mike a message - to tell him explicitly all the ways he had touched my life. I cannot know for sure where that impulse was coming from. Did we have a soul connection that made me feel when he was at the edge of death? Was I empathically picking up on the transition of someone I had a deep emotional bond with? It was hard for me to see it any other way.

Unable to sit still that night, I walked around my neighbourhood deep in thought. I alternated between feelings of appreciation for Mike and berating myself for not reaching out when I could have. At one point, I was lost in thought, my eyes to the ground, when I nearly walked straight into a streetlamp pole. I was not paying attention to where I was walking and was lucky to have looked up at the very moment before I would have smashed into this obstacle. As I paused, my face inches from the pole, I saw a message someone had written in bold print on its surface at eye level. It read:

NEXT TIME

LISTEN TO YOUR GUT

I stood and stared in disbelief. It felt like Mike was talking to me, telling me exactly what he would have said if we had been sitting on his porch, and I recounted this ordeal to him: *"Your gut was telling you loud and clear, brother. Next time, listen. Never hold back when you feel what you were feeling - this is the most important thing in life."*

With tears in my eyes, I let the message in. Fortunately for me, there would be many more next times.

Four

A few days after receiving the news about Mike's death, I got a phone call from Maya. We had been taking a break from talking, hoping that time and space would help us both begin moving on. It had been a week or so since we last spoke, and to my surprise, that brief time apart had made space for a change: Maya was calling to let me know she had met someone new and was extremely excited about him. She felt she had to tell me this out of respect or integrity - to keep me up to speed on this sudden, seismic change in her world. After she shared her update, we said goodbye, and I wished her the best with her budding new romance.

As I processed this conversation, I realized that Maya had moved on, just like that. I'd ended our relationship, and now it was really over - she had found someone else. I felt the sting of this reality and couldn't comprehend how it happened so fast. It left me reeling.

But instead of dwelling on my loneliness, I forced myself to look forward. Over the following weeks, I began going to the gym more than ever, taking the frustration and sadness I felt and channelling them into the primal aggression of lifting weights.

I also began looking for ways to push myself out of my shell - to step into new and scary social situations, meet people, and experience life beyond my isolation. Admitting that I was lonely, didn't know what to do about it, and needed to go out into new places seeking connection with strangers made me feel sick.

My first attempt at stepping out of my shell was to start attending local meetup groups. These were free public events focused on a specific theme or area of interest. I found a group for creatives (writers, artists, etc.) that I decided to check out, and I mostly sat in silence, observing as others spoke.

Part of this event involved a circle format of sharing and discussion, where a question was asked to the group and answered by each participant as we sat in a circle together, listening. The question we were given was: *What lesson are you learning about expressing yourself in the world?*

I liked the question, and after a moment of thought, I found my answer: Shame and insecurity kept me from expressing myself and stepping into the world naturally and honestly. They'd almost kept me from coming to sit in this circle with these strangers. I was learning how to push beyond them.

When it was my turn to speak, I openly shared this thought. I didn't hold back - I gave a voice to my fears (and the yearning for life that contradicted them). When I finished speaking, I immediately felt embarrassed and ashamed. I'd shared more than anyone else there. I'd talked too long, said too much, and shrunk into my seat, wishing I could erase what had just happened. I felt like a child who wanted to disappear.

Then, a woman sitting across from me in the circle spoke: "That's exactly how I feel," she remarked. She proceeded to launch into a confession of her challenges, inhibitions, and insecurities.

Other individuals in the circle began echoing similar experiences or feelings - and it suddenly seemed like I hadn't made such a horrible fool of myself after all. It almost seemed like the opposite was true.

After the meetup event that night, I walked home buzzing with a natural high - a euphoric feeling that I had gone somewhere and exposed a part of myself, and it had been good. People liked it, and it brought something bright to a tiny corner of the world. This was a heavenly elixir for the insecurity in me that wanted to hide from judgment and rejection.

After that night, I started finding other meetup groups I could attend. I looked into different clubs and hobbies I could try. Every opportunity for social connection I thought of or found felt awkward and scary, but that seemed to be the point - that was the medicine I needed.

It looked like this would be the chapter of my life when I finally embraced the world and forced myself into connection with people in ways I had long avoided. Everything was in place, including my willingness to step outside the confines of my comfort zone. Then, before I could barely get started, everything stopped.

This was the winter of 2020. As I prepared to launch into a new chapter of worldly experiences, all public activity came grinding to a halt. Vague rumours about a mysterious illness became a global emergency within a few weeks. My work closed its doors, along with every other place of public activity or social engagement, and I found myself locked down alone in my apartment - in complete isolation. As soon as I was ready to say *yes* to the world - to push myself into society with reckless abandon - it shut down.

My first few weeks in lockdown were surprisingly enjoyable. Because I had spent so many years in solitude, this experience of isolation wasn't altogether different or challenging. There was even something satisfying about knowing so many others were going through the same thing at that moment. For the first time, I wasn't an oddball loner - nearly everyone was playing a version of this game of solitude.

The most fortunate thing to happen during the early days of the lockdown was my developing headaches which stopped me from using my phone and computer. For years, I'd had an on-again, off-again issue with a type of pressure headache that happened when I used electronic devices excessively (usually my smartphone or laptop), especially when that excessive use coincided with periods of emotional stress. During my first days of isolation, I recklessly overdid my smartphone and laptop use and had a flare-up of my old symptoms. Because of this, I decided to take an extended break from staring at any device with a screen to let my nervous system calm down and recover.

Without constant technological distractions, I had to find something to do with my endless free time. I knew that to stay sane in isolation, I needed to get outside and into nature, so I began to take long walks along the ocean and in the large, forested nature park near my apartment every day. With little else to do, walking among the trees and by the waterside became the central feature of my daily life.

These walks almost always began with me feeling depressed or hopeless about my endless loneliness and the stupidity of life. Then, an hour or two later, after breathing the ocean air, being surrounded by trees, moving my body, and reflecting on my anxieties, I felt great. It was such a consistent, pronounced result that I latched onto these walks as a lifeline. Somehow I could enter that forest every morning feeling like shit and leave it an hour later with eyes wide open in awe at the beauty of life. It was a daily renewal - a tonic. I wasn't sure how I'd ever lived without it.

One day, sitting alone in my apartment, I decided to do some writing. I was still abstaining from using my computer, so I found an old electronic typewriter device I'd bought years earlier and never used. It was essentially a full-sized keyboard with a tiny screen (not unlike the dull, grey screen of a pocket calculator) that only showed a few lines of text as I typed. Designed for writers in the field who wanted a small, portable device to write on, it also provided an elegant solution for those who wanted to work without the temptations or distractions of using a computer with internet access.

When I sat down in my apartment to play around on this keyboard, there was an instant outpouring of words, and I was swept into a current of creativity. It had been so long since I did anything creative just for the heck of it, that a well of pent-up energy and excitement burst as soon as I made a little space for it to flow. When I finally pulled myself away from writing to eat something and go outside, I felt high.

Going for a bike ride by the water, it felt like I'd just taken an excellent drug - one that made the world glow, and made me feel like I was going to explode with excitement. I wanted to scream at the sky, I had so much energy.

My days soon revolved around writing. I would wake up, walk in the woods, write for a while, swim in the ocean, and write again. Then repeat. It was as though I had awakened a sleeping force in me - a creative energy I had neglected for years, and feeling it move freely was life-changing. I had no idea if what I was writing during these days was actually good, but I knew how it felt to be doing it - it felt like the best thing ever. I quickly realized that what I was creating could become a book, and I committed to writing it from start to finish. Given the conditions of life at that moment, it was the perfect time for such an intensely solitary undertaking.

As my writing continued, so did the sensation of being high. On my daily walks, I felt an energy moving through my body. Sometimes it was a giddiness, a euphoria, or a warmth glowing in my chest. It was not subtle. It was something I had felt before, and in nearly the same way, but under very different circumstances: It felt like I was falling in love with a woman. The swooning, euphoric glow buzzing through my body was something I had experienced in the early stages of a passionate romantic relationship. There was a spring in my step, a renewed sense of aliveness, and a constant feeling of affection - the classic symptoms of a nascent love affair. Yet I had been sitting alone in my apartment typing at a keyboard.

This glowing feeling continued to build as I continued to write. My body kept presenting the symptoms of a burgeoning new love - an energy or chemistry that grew stronger the longer I worked on this book. Because there was so little to distract me from a steady, creative flow, this state remained uninterrupted. I swam in the salty ocean multiple times a day. I rode my bike along the water. I walked in the forest among the plants and animals. It was all very romantic.

During this time, I remembered something my Dad said to me when I was eighteen years old. We were driving in his car together, talking about what I was going to do with my life. He told me: "You're the kind of person that always has to be making something to be happy, Miles. You have to be creating something - you have to be creative - or it won't be good."

I didn't think my Dad knew what he was talking about at the time and disagreed - I was convinced that he didn't understand me at all. But with the rush of energy and aliveness I was now feeling (after years of living without this kind of creative activity), I realized that he must have been seeing me clearly - more clearly than I had seen myself. I needed to engage in creation if this was what it felt like. It seemed like no amount of emotional work, self-analysis, or positive reinforcement could do what the creative act was doing to me.

After nearly two months, the initial lockdown began to ease. My workplace reopened, and I returned to my job (waiting on tables in a restaurant) part-time. People began socializing more freely, and I realized I could return to a somewhat regular life if I wanted to. I could go on dates, meet up with friends, and have a glimmer of a social life. But because I'd tapped into such a fruitful creative zone, I decided to remain in solitude voluntarily and finish what I started. I had hit a vein of productivity and flow, and the prospect of splitting my attention away from that (by, for example, becoming infatuated with a beautiful woman) seemed negligent. Afraid of losing the focus and drive I had stumbled into, I opted to stay in isolation.

I promised myself that as soon as the first draft of this book was done, I could start dating again and embrace a more social life. But once I reached that goal and completed my first draft, I had so much more work to do that it still seemed foolish to entertain worldly distractions.

So as the world reopened, I stayed in lockdown. For the next seven months, I divided my time between evening shifts waiting on tables, lengthy writing sessions, walks in the woods, swimming in the ocean, and the occasional meetup with a friend outdoors.

There was a fiery, passionate intensity to this process. It was a feeling that made my fear of missing out on life dissolve. When I went for evening walks alone by the water and watched countless lovers stroll past me in each others' arms, I felt no pangs of jealousy. I was not confronted by the harsh reality of my loneliness and solitude. As far as I was concerned, I wasn't alone. In the same way that a person touches something mysterious, unknown, and sacred in the beauty of their lover, writing was an act of communion with something profound that balanced me and made my incompleteness feel whole. It made my world feel alive with something greater than myself.

I spent warm summer days indoors at a keyboard, happy. Then fall days poring over a manuscript, refining and editing it endlessly. I daydreamed about it, was moved by it, and fantasized about it. Part of this process was almost constantly painful - pushing past my insecurities, procrastination, and the heavy weight of inner criticism. But on the other side of that pain was something glorious.

Nine months after beginning work on my book, it was complete. It was December now, and I quietly self-published my labour of love to an audience of a few friends, coworkers, and individuals who followed me after discovering writing I had published a decade earlier. I had no idea how people would react to what I created in my bubble of isolation, but I knew that I loved it.

After publishing that book, there was an initial sense of relief. I felt I'd finished the hard part of a journey and could relax. It quickly became apparent, however, that the hard part had not ended. A new chapter of challenges had just begun.

Spending time writing by myself for months on end was challenging, but it was also very safe. After all, I was creating my own world within the confines of my apartment. Now that something tangible had been produced from that introspective activity, I had to stand up and tell people about it. I had to draw attention to my work. I had to come out of hiding. It was like I'd set a trap for myself that would push me out of my shell and force my insecurity to get in front of strangers and be witnessed by their harsh gaze.

One day before work, I was getting changed with some coworkers when one of them asked me what the book I had just written was about. His tone was sincere, warm, and curious.

But before I could think about his question, I froze in embarrassment. It was like someone had injected me with an intravenous dose of pure, unrefined shame. I was so self-conscious and insecure about the work I'd just shared with the world that the mere mention of it caused me to seize up in fear.

After a few moments of silently scrambling for words, I said: "Um... it's hard to describe. I guess it's about the ego - learning about the ego."

My answer was so strained, uncomfortable, and awkward that his only response was to take a step back with a look of confusion (bordering on concern) and say: "Um...okay."

He had been asking about my book because he was sincerely interested in it - but I was so uncomfortable sharing this part of myself with others that I had given him perhaps the worst sales pitch possible. Instead of joyfully opening up and talking about this work that I loved and was proud of, my shame and defensiveness sent him a clear message: GO AWAY. PLEASE DON'T LOOK AT ME.

Unfortunately, my defensiveness did a fantastic job - that was the last time he ever asked about the book. I effectively pushed him away.

Another coworker wasn't so easily dissuaded. She asked for a copy of the book one afternoon as we were getting ready before work, on a day when I happened to have a copy of it in my bag. Before I could trip over my words and scare her away, she had the book in her hands and declared: "This is perfect timing! I needed a book to read this week, and now I have yours, Miles. Life just works out some days."

The next time I saw her (about a week later), she approached me mid-shift and said: "Miles, we need to talk about your book."

I was nervous to hear her feedback as I asked her what she thought of it.

"Miles, it's so beautiful. I honestly needed to read that in this lifetime."

Her words were a surprise and a relief. We spoke about the book at length and continued discussing it over the following months. After reading that book, she knew a lot about me, and through these conversations, I began to learn all sorts of moving things about her.

Soon, another coworker read it, then another. People at work started to know who my old friend Kevin was and would make jokes about him. Others would ask me for copies of the book because they heard it was good.

The effect of this was that, over time, I became comfortable talking with strangers about my writing (and myself). That workplace was almost like a laboratory - a social space I went to routinely that triggered patterns of insecurity and hiding, and gave me the opportunity to outgrow them. This couldn't be done through introspection - it wasn't something I could do alone or even with a lover or trusted friend. The social, public nature of that workplace - the random assortment of characters I wouldn't know or be connected to otherwise - seemed to be an ideal lab for this experiment.

Over several months, I noticed that what began as a chokehold of awkwardness and discomfort when someone asked me what my book was about slowly relaxed. I began to understand how to describe my creation more clearly as my emotional triggering mellowed. And as I got feedback about it from individuals that ranged from eighteen-year-old girls to ninety-year-old men, I realized that it wasn't so weird or hard to explain to the average person. It was an honest story about someone exploring love and vulnerability in their day-to-day life. It wasn't that odd - it was just me.

The book did not explode into a bestselling sensation overnight. Instead, it reached my tiny network of friends and acquaintances and then rested at the edge of that bubble.

As time passed, the number of copies the book sold was small, but the response it evoked in some of those readers was dramatic. This was a complicated reality for my brain to digest: Materially, the book consistently performed much worse than I had expected. My audience grew one person at a time, not by hundreds or thousands overnight. But at some deep level, everything about this seemed brilliant.

Looking at other successful authors or influencers could make me feel disheartened and embarrassed at my current reality. As I played with finding my voice through podcasting and other mediums, it sometimes felt like I was creating work to send out into empty space - more as a way of feeding a spiritual need within myself than sharing work with an audience. It often seemed that there wasn't anyone listening, but I felt that I had to do it regardless.

Here and there, I would get messages from strangers so strong they pushed me forward. These messages seemed like strange glimmers of light, with long stretches of emptiness between them. They were often perfectly timed to flash into my life at just the right moment to encourage me and push me along on a path that sometimes felt totally irrational - but also like the only way forward.

I was well aware during this period that my lack of material success as an author was a very healthy thing - almost a tonic. There was a humility that my situation asked of me: To carry on with a path that did not produce instant results. To believe in a vision regardless of response or validation from the world around me. To accept my position as being less than others - at least in some crude, superficial way. Or even better: To embrace it.

Four

As I owned my humbling reality, something about it did start to feel exciting. I was *hungry*, and I wasn't established, polished or successful. Not only was there nothing wrong with that, there was something wildly invigorating about it.

In moments of doubt, a voice would come into my head and say: *"This is a test, Miles. Will you have faith? Will you continue when the path isn't easy or instant? Will you give up when the world doesn't hand you what you want, or will you hold the vision? Will you do the work? How devoted are you to this?"*

Five

As I finished work on my new book, I met a young woman named Ayana. Ayana went to the same gym as me, where we first crossed paths. During the lockdown (and for several months following it), I stopped going to the gym, and I found it hard to bring myself back there after taking that time away. My new routine of walking in the forest made visiting the gym far less appealing than it had previously been - I was now used to a practice of moving my body that involved being surrounded by the perfect beauty of the natural world, so the gym's artificial, stuffy ambience didn't quite measure up. Still, I wanted to stay in shape, so I eventually convinced myself to renew my monthly membership.

It had been about six months since my last visit by the time I finally dragged myself back to the gym. Although being there wasn't comparable to being out in the woods, it was fun to use all of the equipment again and to see some familiar faces grinding away as they had been the last time I was there. I knew a few regulars and had brief conversations with them occasionally, but for the most part, I didn't socialize when I was at the gym. One factor in this was the antisocial intensity of working out. Another factor was a form of respect for others - I didn't want to interrupt their flow. I felt this even more so with women. In a way, I saw the gym as a sacred space for women. I could see how annoying it might be for an attractive female to have unsolicited attention directed at her from men while minding her own business, so I had firm boundaries with this. I tried to give women plenty of space. I would do my best to be kind and courteous, but I turned off my sexual or romantic self at the gym. It seemed like an unspoken rule to follow and meant that I rarely conversed with women within those hallowed walls, and kept things very simple if such an interaction occurred.

On my first visit back to the gym, I was stretching when I noticed a beautiful woman across the room beaming an enormous smile and waving in my direction. I looked up at her bright, smiling face and felt confused. This gorgeous woman was looking toward me and waving with wide-eyed excitement. I looked behind me to see who she was waving at, but no one was obvious - I saw a handful of people preoccupied with their workouts and looking down at their phones. When I looked back toward her, she had turned around and walked into a change room.

After a few moments of confusion, I wondered: *Was she waving at me? Did I just completely ignore that absurdly beautiful woman?* The answer was yes. If she had been waving at me, I responded with a complete lack of acknowledgment, turning away and ignoring her gesture of wide-open kindness. I was somewhat horrified by how I fumbled that so badly.

During my next visit to the gym, I nearly crashed straight into that same woman while walking through a hallway. Both of us had been distracted while walking toward each other, looking to the side or down at a phone instead of watching where we were going, and a second before we would have otherwise collided, we looked up, stopped in our tracks, and met eyes. Maybe because of the suddenness and surprise, a wall that I typically would have had up wasn't in place, and when my eyes met with this woman's, I found myself staring into them in awe. For a moment, we stood in silence - before laughing, apologizing, and carrying on our way.

It was a fleeting interaction. We had exchanged almost no words. And yet something significant was said non-verbally during it. It felt like we were both caught off guard, and before either of our personalities or defensive masks could engage, our eyes communicated a simple message directly to one another. At that moment, I caught a glimpse of something beautiful - an energy or chemistry like a fire it was so intense. I needed to know who this person was.

After that run-in, I began going to the gym more frequently. I knew I was doing this with the hope of running into that woman again. Maybe, if the timing was right, we would naturally find ourselves in a conversation, and I could get a sense of who she was and if what I had felt in that moment of connection had any translation to real life.

I knew this was all a flagrant violation of my number one rule at the gym: *Don't bother women*. But I hadn't felt this spark in such a long time that I had to find out more - I had to break the rule.

With these things in mind, I started exchanging smiles and hellos with this mysterious woman more frequently. Our schedules lined up often, as I saw her nearly every time I visited the gym. And every time we said hello, I felt my heart pounding, accompanied by a dizzying nervous excitement. Her beauty moved me in a way that reminded me of the immensity of an ancient, old-growth forest - I saw something supernatural, otherworldly, and humbling in her. In a world of humdrum, mediocre humanity, she glowed with an energy that was magnificent and inspiring. She seemed different - open, strong, dignified, and kind. All of this is to say that I had a crush.

One day while I was working out, she came to stretch beside me, and my heart almost exploded. I couldn't believe what was happening. I'd been building up such a dramatic suspense and infatuation around this woman that I had to take a few deep breaths before I forced myself to say hello. After exchanging an awkward greeting, we quickly slipped into a conversation.

I remember little of what we spoke about - I was so excited it's a blur. At one point, I asked how she had been doing with the lockdown over the past few months. The two of us shared how we'd both struggled with the isolation and found ways of dealing with it - and how it had made us grateful for little things we previously took for granted.

I acknowledged that I had been seeing her at the gym for a while, yet this was the first time we truly spoke. I took the opportunity to introduce myself, and she shared that her name was Ayana. She then shook my hand and told me it was great to have a conversation finally.

After we said goodbye, I stumbled out of the gym in complete awe of what had just transpired. Not only had I finally managed to talk with Ayana, but she also seemed quite open to me. She seemed like she was gushing with happiness the whole time we spoke. Her eyes were glowing, and her voice was full of excitement. I almost couldn't believe or let in what had just happened - she had acted like someone very excited to be talking with me.

As I walked onto the busy street in front of the gym, the evening sky caught my attention. The clouds had taken on a warm, pink glow from the light of the setting sun. Below them, there was a bright rainbow stretching across the horizon. At that moment, the display of light and colour above me seemed like a perfect reflection of my feelings.

I couldn't help but make some meaning out of the timing of this rainbow. I'd finally spoken to Ayana, and immediately afterwards, there was this symbol of wish fulfillment - a sign of miracles and hope. I wondered to myself if this was the heavens rejoicing.

After that initial conversation with Ayana, we began chatting whenever we saw one another. Every time we spoke, she seemed incredibly open and warm - and I found myself more drawn to her. I was unsure how to proceed, aside from seizing any opportunity to talk with her that presented itself.

On my way to work one day, I was thinking about throwing my reservations to the side and asking Ayana - respectfully and politely - if she wanted to grab a coffee or go for a walk together sometime. While I imagined this course of action, my gaze drifted to the sky, and I noticed a double rainbow hovering above the city.

My eyes almost jumped out of my face as I let the image I was staring at sink in. *Another rainbow? Right now?*

It felt like I was receiving some kind of divine encouragement - a confirmation from the sky that there was something right about connecting with Ayana. I knew that whatever chemistry I felt with her was extremely rare - it had been a decade since I had last felt anything like it, and I knew it might be another decade before I stumbled into it again. So I began to steel myself against the awkwardness of my only rational course of action: I would have to ask a woman out. The thought of it made me nauseous.

Despite my fear of rejection and embarrassment, I had no choice but to shoot my shot with Ayana. Over the following days, I looked for opportunities to ask if she wanted to hang out sometime - I waited for the right moment.

During one of our conversations, Ayana found out that I had published a book and asked if she could buy a copy from me. I was excited for her to have one and offered to give it to her as a gift the next time we saw each other. I realized that this could be what facilitated our connecting on another level. Ayana would read my book, and then we could hang out and talk about it. It was perfect.

The next time I went to the gym, I brought a copy of my book and put it in a locker with my belongings. When I saw Ayana, I grabbed it and gave it to her. She was beaming with excitement, and we sat down to talk for a few minutes about my process writing it and her favourite authors.

Before we finished our chat, she handed me a pen and asked if I would sign the book. I was happy to do this - the only problem was that my hands began shaking so much from my nervousness I couldn't write. I'd never experienced this kind of debilitating excitement around a woman. Because of it, she got a barely legible signature - it looked like it had been scribbled by a five-year-old using their non-dominant hand.

Ayana didn't seem to notice or care about my visible trembling as I signed the book and handed it back to her. We exchanged a few more words, shared a warm goodbye, and carried along our separate ways. Now that Ayana had my book, it seemed inevitable that we would speak more and that whatever connection was possible between us would reveal itself soon.

Throughout all of this, I was becoming aware of something slightly unsettling, and my uncontrollable shaking hands were just one small manifestation of it: I felt weak in relation to Ayana. There was a sense of smallness, fear, and insecurity that I experienced whenever I was near her, which troubled me. To the degree that I felt her grandeur, strength, and immense beauty, I shrunk. As I recognized what was happening, I asked myself how I could lose my confidence, composure, and strength so quickly in her presence? How could this woman, who I knew nothing about, reduce me to a breathless, dazed and nervous child in an instant? There was something here for me to learn.

When I spoke to Pandora about my fascination with Ayana, she wanted to see a photo of this crush of mine. So we looked at Ayana's social media profiles together, and I asked Pandora for her impressions. A perceptive and intuitive woman, I knew Pandora's thoughts would be interesting.

"Well, she's gorgeous," Pandora observed. "I can see why you're drawn to her. But - - I don't know if she could see *you*."

Pandora furrowed her brow and took a moment to process something in silence before continuing. "Yeah, I'm not sure if she could see what makes you special. It's like she doesn't have that on her radar - like, she couldn't see the beauty in your vulnerability - the magic of who you are. Yeah, I'm not convinced she could see that at all."

After another moment of silent reflection, she added: "I could be wrong. I hope that I'm wrong!"

I looked at the images Pandora had just been scrolling through, and I hoped that she was wrong, too.

About a week after I gave Ayana my book, I saw her again. She came up to me in the middle of a workout and struck up a conversation. Near the end of our interaction, she mentioned that she'd started reading my book but only got as far as the first few pages, so she had nothing to share about it yet.

"I'll have to read more of it before I give you my honest review," she said.

My thinking may have been distorted by pride and ego here, but this information immediately concerned me. If I had gotten my hands on a book Ayana wrote that was a personal story, I would have read it from cover to cover in one sitting. My rational mind couldn't help but register her lack of progress with the book as a sign of disinterest. After all, I'd heard from strangers who had read it in one afternoon. If Ayana was interested in me (in the way I was interested in her), wouldn't she have blazed through it by now?

I didn't rest with these thoughts for long, though. Ayana was still warm and felt open to me when we spoke. We were developing a familiarity that seemed sincere and beautiful. A little sign of disinterest wasn't going to scare me off.

At this point, I decided it was time to make a direct move. I gave Ayana the book, and we started becoming more friendly. Now, I had to take the next step. I knew I had to do this tactfully, but the time had come.

There had already been a dozen moments when I wanted to confessionally gush to Ayana about everything I felt - to share my admiration for her and the enormous, beautiful energy she had awakened in me. But every time I went to take a step in this direction, something stopped me. I could feel how such a confession would backfire. I could feel how Ayana would not be receptive to such a vulnerable display of emotions. I sensed it would freak her out and scare her away.

In the past, my experience was that such vulnerability had been received well by the few women I shared it with - they loved the transparency. But something about Ayana was different. And for some reason, I liked that.

It meant that I had to contain the torrential feelings swooning inside me. It meant that instead of sharing everything I was going through and getting validation from the focus of my affection, I had to hold it all for myself. There was no reassurance from the woman I had become fascinated by. There was no sense of relief after impulsively sharing the burden of my feelings with another. There was pain, discomfort, and the discipline of containment. It felt good. It felt like a weak part of me that wanted reassurance was being forced to contain itself. An impetuous, self-conscious boy was being asked to behave like a patient, self-respecting man.

So rather than passionately divulging everything I was going through to Ayana, I composed myself. I waited for the right moment the next time I saw her, and after pushing through a wall of insecurity, I made my move.

The timing was perfect: I waited until I finished my workout, put my jacket on, and was ready to make my way out of the gym. Ayana was sitting on a piece of equipment near the exit, meaning that if I approached her there, the moment I finished making a fool of myself, I could vanish through the front door.

After readying myself with a few deep breaths, I made my move. As I walked past her on my way out, I casually said: "Hey Ayana - I've really been enjoying getting to know you a bit lately. I'm curious to know more about you and your life, and if you're ever interested, I would love to grab a coffee or go for a walk sometime."

I couldn't believe how smoothly I strung those words together. A big smile broke across Ayana's face, and she responded: "I would love that, Miles!"

Her hands came together in the shape of a prayer in front of her chest as she enthusiastically accepted my offer, and we made a tentative plan to meet for coffee and a walk soon. I then turned and nearly ran for the exit - I was beside myself with excitement.

Ayana and I met up the following Wednesday. After a couple of last-minute changes due to her schedule, we ended up at a popular neighbourhood breakfast place so she could get something to eat while we hung out.

After we sat down and shared how our days had been going, the conversation took off. For the most part, I asked Ayana questions about her life, passions, relationships, etc. As she shared stories and experiences, I stared with wide-eyed awe, becoming even more impressed and infatuated with this stunning woman.

Ayana had very few questions for me. Most of our conversation involved my sitting in quiet reverence as she spoke. The few times I did talk about my life, I felt a palpable sense of judgment from Ayana. It was a curious twist to everything, but as I sat across from her with an endless curiosity and wide-open, awestruck heart, she gave me the impression that she was closed off. She had an air of distance and disinterest, coolly studying me with a stern, discerning gait, not quite sure what to think of this dude. It felt like I was seeing her as a goddess, and she was seeing me as a suspiciously mediocre, unaccomplished, sub-average guy.

When she got a work-related text and had to rush back to her apartment and take care of some business, I offered to walk there with her. As we walked and spoke, she seemed more open again and shared how excited she was to get to know me more. When we arrived at her place, she asked if she could hug me and said: "I'm really grateful for this friendship."

I smiled, thanked her for the conversation, and stumbled away, more infatuated and confused than before. Ayana's gratitude for my *friendship* seemed like it might be a death blow to my dream of something more. And the feeling I had of being judged while we sat in the diner together was not exactly fun to experience. But I could not be discouraged so easily.

Instead of overthinking the mixed messages I had just received, I trusted that the truth would reveal itself soon enough if I took more steps down this path.

A few days after that visit, I contacted Ayana and asked if she would like to get together again. She was wide open and quick to accept my invitation, and we met for a walk along the ocean on a sunny afternoon that weekend. As we began our walk together, Ayana shared a situation she was struggling with involving a male friend who had fallen in love with her. She valued the presence of this man in her life, but when he confessed that he wanted to be more than friends, she made it clear to him that nothing of that nature would ever happen - she didn't feel that way about him. Once it became evident to this man that his feelings were not reciprocated, he chose to stop torturing himself and ended their connection. Ayana was disappointed and confused by the loss of this friend and wished they could somehow maintain their relationship.

As she spoke, I wondered if I was receiving a gift from the heavens - because it seemed like I was about to suffer the same fate as this naive, love-struck friend Ayana had just described. I appeared to be the next fool in line who thought he had a chance of being more than friends with her.

Instead of feeling insecure or trying to change the subject, I started laughing at myself and thought it might be the perfect moment to clarify my intentions.

"Ayana, I think I have to take this opportunity to acknowledge what's happening," I said. "Honestly, I might be doing the same thing as the friend you just described. So, let me be obvious: I'm interested in you in a way that is not strictly platonic - not at all. And, as you were speaking, I realized that I'm probably about to repeat this story with you. I obviously don't really know you well yet - and I'm not jumping ahead of myself, but I am interested in you in a more-than-friendly way. And if you already know that isn't how you feel about me, that's totally fine. I can accept that and would respect it…"

Ayana interrupted me before I could finish: "No, Miles. It's not the same! I *want* you to feel that way about me. I like it - it's different."

Ayana was laughing now, too.

She insisted that our situation wasn't anything like the story she'd just told, but I wasn't entirely convinced. After all, she still hadn't exactly reciprocated my interest in her - she had merely acknowledged that it felt nice to receive. But this seemed to be her style - where I was transparent and direct, she was slow-moving, hesitant, complex, and secretive. It was strangely attractive.

We continued walking along the water and chatting for some time before I offered to accompany her back to her apartment. When we arrived there, she asked me if I wanted to come up and hang out for a while. Trying to hide my nervous excitement, I said yes.

When we entered her place, she offered me a drink, and we sat in her living room. I navigated my awkwardness by looking at her bookshelf, noticing books I had read or recognized, and making small talk about them. Ayana may have been trying to navigate her awkwardness with a drink.

As we sat together in the quiet intimacy of her apartment, I noticed that instead of feeling an insatiable chemistry with Ayana, I felt an emotional wall separating us. It was confusing - she was incredibly physically attractive, but there seemed to be something blocking a sense of attraction and chemistry between us.

When she invited me up to her apartment, I had assumed we would probably kiss, but given what I was feeling, there was no chance of that happening. We sat together in that living room but felt very far apart.

Typically, I would have brought this up and openly acknowledged my feelings. But when I tried to do this, something stopped me from speaking. I couldn't get the words to form - the sentences fell apart before they made it out of my mouth.

After spending a few minutes in her apartment, Ayana addressed the wall I could feel between us.

During a break in our conversation, she said: "Maybe I'm too closed to love. I have some pretty big walls up. Maybe I should think about taking them down. I'm very slow to open - there's just - - a lot going on. I'm very - - guarded. It's just - - it's complicated."

She spoke with exasperation, like someone who'd been carrying a burden for a long time. We were sitting on separate chairs as she said these words, and after she finished speaking, I simply looked into her eyes and nodded. Again, I wanted to say something to encourage her to open up, to push through the wall separating us, but I felt like I was being stopped, and I assumed this meant that she had to move at her own pace.

After talking for a while, I excused myself so that Ayana could get ready to meet with a friend for dinner that night. We exchanged a hug and said a warm goodbye.

Walking home, I was convinced that something would happen between us the next time we hung out. Ayana seemed to require patience in her process, and I was more than willing to give it. All good things are worth waiting for.

Shortly after that visit, Ayana got sick and had to self-isolate for a week. I offered to bring her groceries or anything else she needed, but she insisted that was unnecessary. Over the following days and weeks, I checked in with her by sending text messages periodically, seeing how she was doing, and offering words of kindness and support.

After she recovered and was back to life as usual, I reached out to see if she would like to hang out again. She responded with an enthusiastic yes, after which I asked what days and times would work for her.

I didn't think much of it when she didn't respond immediately. People get busy. But then a couple of days passed with no response. Then a week passed with no word from her, and I could barely contain the anxious feeling in my gut.

Ayana might have gotten distracted by life. She might have thought she responded. Or, she might not want to connect after all. Being in the awkward place of opening up to rejection and having life hit the *pause* button there for a week was somewhat torturous. But good things are worth waiting for, I reminded myself. So I contained my vulnerability, and when the time felt right, I reached out again.

Instead of asking Ayana why she hadn't responded, I kept things simple and asked her how she was doing. Her response was immediate and almost confusingly warm. She said she was excited to hear from me and had been thinking about me a lot, which I found confusing, but was happy to hear.

After exchanging a few messages, I asked if she wanted to connect in person, and she replied with an immediate, enthusiastic yes. When I asked what days or times would work best for her, the conversation ended abruptly - she didn't respond.

Again, I realized that people get busy - life happens. Then a day passed, and I wondered if the same thing was occurring again. Then a few more days passed without a response, and I was in awe of this pattern repetition.

A week after this latest message to Ayana, still having received no response, I worked up the courage to reach out to her again. In the past, if a woman had rebuffed my advances even slightly, I would have turned around and walked away. I had too much pride and impatience to continue knocking on someone's door if they weren't going to meet me and match my enthusiasm. But good things are worth waiting for, I told myself. So I chose to knock again. As strange as this situation was starting to feel, I liked the aspect of my personality that it was bringing out: A part of me capable of patience - capable of waiting for something worthwhile.

Again, I determined the best move would be to ignore the awkward lapse in our conversation and simply ask Ayana how she was doing. I went ahead with this, and her response was immediate and warm. She expressed how excited she was to hear from me, and again, I was confused.

When I eventually asked if she would like to get together soon, she responded with an enthusiastic yes. I followed up by asking when would work for her and waited for her response.

A few hours passed, and I wondered if she was busy. Then days passed - still no response. Then a week, and I was in disbelief. The silent rejection I had been experiencing was repeating itself once more. But it started to feel different.

There was something about Ayana that I could not give up on easily. What I had felt in her presence was too rare, too extraordinary. It seemed irrational to walk away, even when she ghosted me repeatedly. But just over a week after this latest bizarre interaction, my interest in her vanished. The energy I had been feeling for months - the euphoric attraction and infatuation I had been high on - died. No thought process was attached to this - no intellectual evaluation or discernment. My body was just done with it, over it. Whatever flame had been burning in me went out, and I felt relieved.

By this point, my visits to the gym had become infrequent. Given the strange lapses in communication I was experiencing with Ayana, the public run-ins I had previously hoped for became something I would rather avoid.

Weeks passed, and as I accepted that Ayana was repeatedly ghosting me, I decided it would be best to stop going to that gym entirely. While I was strangely at peace with how things had unfolded, I didn't want to subject myself to the awkwardness or embarrassment of running into Ayana after making somewhat of a fool of myself in front of her. I had broken the first and most sacred rule of the gym - perhaps it was only fitting that I remove myself from it after my transgression. With this in mind, I contacted the gym and cancelled my monthly membership.

In the days and weeks that followed, I was perplexed by what had just happened. There were no feelings of resentment towards Ayana or even disappointment. Instead, I felt a mixture of gratitude and wonder. I was grateful that despite a bizarre lack of communication, I had found an answer to my question about whether or not Ayana was interested in me: Her lack of words spoke clearly.

I also wondered why I had felt such a strong pull to her in the first place? If this is where that pull led me (a slow, quiet rejection), had I been delusional to think something significant was here?

I remembered those initial feelings of fiery, soulful connection. Then, the strange signs that seemed to encourage me - the rainbows, Ayana's gushing, effusive warmth - everything. During long, solitary walks, I reflected on this question, and the answer always seemed to be right in my face: There was something perfect about this rejection.

There was something about everything I experienced with Ayana - my childlike sense of inferiority, the necessity of containing my feelings rather than impulsively heaving them outward and scaring her away, the feeling of being unseen and the slow, awkward rejection - that altogether was working some kind of magic on me. It was like a perfect cocktail crafted to wake up slumbering parts of my being. By not getting love from her, I was forced to look at the places in myself that felt most starved for it. I was forced to find the love somewhere else.

Five

I felt the nervous trembling in my hands. I heard the voices of shame and insecurity ringing in my head. I was forced to sit with all of this and hold it. Because she didn't open up to me, I had to. In this way, I could not have asked for something more perfect or beautiful. I never did get to say any of this to Ayana, but her appearance in my world had been a more brilliant blessing than anything I could have imagined.

Six

I met Kevin's parents about six months after he died. They were visiting Vancouver to collect, organize, and get rid of all the belongings he had left behind. Perhaps they also came to get a tiny glimpse of the life their son had lived during his final years. As they grieved, maybe seeing Kevin's things, and talking to a couple of the people he had been close to, could help them make sense of something senseless: The loss of their son.

It was a sunny summer afternoon when we met at Kevin's old apartment building, where they had been sorting through a storage locker filled with his possessions for the previous two days. My first impression was that they were unbelievably kind, welcoming, and warm. They were also in a moment of devastation. Kevin's mother was beyond heartbroken - raw, vulnerable, barely containing a stream of tears and emotion. His father was a bit more collected, but there was no hiding how massive the pain of all this was for them.

After introducing ourselves, we found a cafe to sit at together and spoke for an hour or so. We shared simple stories about Kevin. We laughed at little things that only those who knew him would comprehend. We asked each other questions to try and better understand him. I struggled to contain my emotions, and it appeared they did, too.

Kevin was estranged from his family during the years when I knew him. He had chosen to stop speaking to them before we met and maintained that boundary firmly until the end of his life. I do not understand all of the reasons for this, but at its essence seemed to be the belief that he would be better off alone. He wanted to outgrow his origin story, to become free from the inherited patterns that troubled him - and pulling back from his family was part of his way of going about that.

Because of this disconnection, his parents had to grieve two losses: The disappearance of the son who had rejected them years earlier - and now, after a long separation, the tragedy of his death.

As we spoke, it became clear that we held memories of Kevin that the other did not know. I had been around Kevin nearly all the time he was estranged from his parents - a chapter of his life that was a mystery to them. And they knew the Kevin who had grown up under their roof. They had watched him become a man. They had seen the power of his brilliance blossom - alongside the demons that haunted him.

Sitting down and talking with his parents that afternoon helped something feel more real about what had happened. It helped me understand that Kevin was gone. During this time, nearly every day, I would see a man riding his bike in the distance and think it was him - I would see someone about Kevin's height walking toward me on the sidewalk and be sure it was my old friend. Some part of my mind hadn't yet accepted that he wasn't here anymore - that I would never see him walking along the sidewalk (or anywhere) again. This meeting was a step toward integrating that reality.

Two things, in particular, stood out during my meeting with Kevin's parents: One was how incredibly loving they were. They adored Kevin and would have done anything for their youngest son. I couldn't help but notice that he had cut that love out of his life.

And I wondered if there might have been a way for him to have done things differently - to have kept that love in his world - and if that might have changed things for the better.

The second thing that struck me was more personal: The heartbreak of Kevin's mother was so intense, savage, and deep that it left me shaken. Near the end of our conversation, she commented on the importance of sons letting their mothers know that they love them - and the importance of me letting my mother know that I love her. In response, I knowingly nodded my head, silently acknowledging the truth of what she was saying.

In a sense, my head-nodding was a lie - because I (like Kevin) had not spoken to my mother in years. Like my old friend, I had chosen to pull away from my parents, albeit in a slightly less dramatic way than he had. At that moment, sitting across from Kevin's grief-stricken mother, this was not something I cared to acknowledge or admit to. But in the days and months that followed, I would not be able to forget the message she delivered:

Tell your mother you love her.

Nearly a year after that meeting with Kevin's parents, Pandora and I were walking along the Vancouver seawall (a beautiful oceanside path) on a bright spring afternoon. During a lull in our conversation, Pandora's voice shifted to a severe and solemn tone, and she said: "I keep on feeling like there's something I need to talk to you about."

With my curiosity piqued, I asked her to share her thoughts.

"It's your family," she continued. "Your parents, in particular. I feel like you need to look at your relationship with them. You have a wall up with your parents that doesn't make sense anymore. It feels like something young in you that wants to grow up. I think that you could get a lot from connecting with them."

My first reaction to Pandora's words was defensiveness. The mere mention of my family made me uncomfortable - but she also seemed to be saying that I was doing something wrong, and my immediate response to that was one of pride. I got standoffish and pushed back.

"I feel sick even thinking about connecting with my parents," I replied. "The idea that I should change my boundaries and open up to them makes no sense. I can't see how it would be a good idea in any way."

"You're proving my point," Pandora calmly responded. "The fact that me mentioning your parents makes you this uncomfortable probably means there's something for you to look at here."

I let myself think before responding: "Hm. I guess you got me."

I admitted that she was likely onto something. Instead of continuing to protect myself from what she was saying, I acknowledged how much it affected me. For the next hour, we spoke about my discomfort and where it might be coming from. Pandora didn't have any strong thoughts or words of advice, just a gut feeling that I needed to reexamine my relationship (or lack thereof) with my parents. She didn't necessarily think I should talk to them, but that I should look, with fresh eyes, at why I *wasn't* talking to them.

After this conversation, an idea at the back of my mind started to grow. I saw how the thought of sitting down to talk with my parents made me feel like an uncomfortable child. I felt how my sense of strength, wisdom, and maturity flew out the window when I returned to my family relationships. And I knew that meant I probably needed to go there.

When I first decided to stop speaking to my family, it wasn't a particularly well thought out choice. My idea was that by pulling away from them, I would have the space to find myself - to grow and heal as a person. Stepping away from complicated, habitual relationships seemed to make perfect sense. It wasn't easy, and I knew it would hurt everyone. Still, I chose to say goodbye to my family guided by courage and determination.

Without realizing it, I was parroting the choices of Kevin - my closest and most influential friend at the time. People can be like drugs - if we spend enough time around them, we might absorb their way of speaking, thinking, and relating to the world. They alter our consciousness. I took on many of Kevin's views and relationship dynamics throughout our friendship without fully understanding what was happening. And in the process, I cut myself off from my family, as he had done before me.

When I broke the news to my family that I was going to disappear from their world, they were surprised and hurt - but respectful. There was a sense of confusion on their part at what had happened for me to make such a bizarre exit from their lives. There had been no argument, no drama, no falling out. I simply told them I would be taking off, that I needed to work on myself, and that they wouldn't be hearing from me indefinitely.

It had been seven years since then, and although I thought about my parents and brothers often, I rarely considered reaching out to them. I had made my choice, and as lonely as it could be, I was committed to it. When

Christmases and birthdays passed, I felt nostalgia and sadness, but I was engaged in a new chapter of life.

I was so focused on emotional work during these years that my family (and my parents in particular) were regular fixtures in my mental landscape, even if it had been ages since we last spoke or saw each other in person. I spent months on end revisiting childhood experiences and unresolved feelings from the past - seeking to better understand myself, where I came from, and why I was who I was.

While my approach was sometimes extreme, an undeniable softening in me came about through it. I sat with some of my feelings of resentment for long enough that they seemed to have screamed and cried themselves to sleep. I looked at my childhood and the emotions surrounding my parents long enough to find a well of understanding and love in me that I did not expect - and it was one of the most beautiful things ever. Much of this happened during the period after Kevin's death - maybe in the emptiness and vulnerability that his absence left, I could find more love and understanding for everyone and everything.

This new sense of inner peace I thought I had found made it all the more jarring when Pandora mentioned my parents, and I seized up in fear. I could tell that whatever peace I thought I had achieved was not fully fleshed out yet. Maybe it had to be held in the complexity of real life - maybe it had to be held with them to become something more substantial. With all of this dawning on me, I began walking in circles around the obvious, awkward task ahead.

Before I could reach out to any of my family members, I had to reconcile with what I put them through. My mother, father, and brothers had all been confused, hurt, and blindsided by my choice to disappear from their worlds. Now, years later, as I readied myself to knock on each of their doors and sheepishly say hello, I took plenty of time to meditate on the consequences of my decisions. Enough life had happened for me to understand how extreme my choice to sever ties with them had been. And what little I had heard from them or found out through the grapevine had given me a sense of the pain I left in my absence.

It seemed there was a tragic irony to what I had done. There was a boy inside me who always felt like he had been a burden. He felt like he had been unwanted or rejected by his family on some deep level. And to deal with these feelings, he had decided to leave his family - he took his inner sense of rejection and inflicted it upon those who loved him the most. And in the end, it didn't help him feel any better.

Without knowing it, I prepared myself to talk with my family by sincerely reflecting on all the reasons to say *sorry*.

I could only walk in circles for so long before it was time to make a move. After some consideration, I decided to begin this process by contacting my brothers. Before disappearing, I had been closest to my younger brother, Lenny. I thought he would be the most sympathetic and understanding of my choices, so I reached out to him first. I sent a short, carefully worded email letting him know I was thinking about him and would be open to talking if he ever wanted to. He responded immediately, giving me his current phone number and inviting me to call anytime.

I called Lenny on a weekday evening when I was off from work. As I dialled his number and let the phone ring, I took a deep breath to calm my racing heart. Then he picked up.

There was a moment of muffled noise and then a voice: "Hey, how's it going?"

I didn't recognize the voice on the other end of the phone. It was confusing, and for a moment, I remained silent - perplexed by who I was talking to and what was happening. I had dialled the number Lenny sent me, and the person who answered was talking as though they were expecting my call - but his voice was not one I recognized.

After a brief silence, I proceeded as though I was talking to my brother. I said hello, asked how things were going, and over several minutes of conversation, it became clear that this was, in fact, Lenny. But he sounded unfamiliar. Something was different - his voice or energy - it wasn't how I remembered. And the difference wasn't subtle - it was jarring. I realized that a lot of life had happened, and the brother I had known must have changed (or maybe I was different).

There was a wall of awkwardness to push through as we navigated our conversation. I tried to break the ice by sharing some of the events that had occurred in my life since we last spoke: The years of solitude and monkish inner work, the poverty, random jobs, and eventually, Kevin's death. I shared how beautiful some parts of my years away had been - the learning, discoveries, and growth. I described the seasons of devastating isolation and neurotic over-analyzing. I humbly acknowledged how my choice to leave his world had been extreme and something that I was now embarrassed by. I apologized to him.

He, in turn, shared a brief update from his world: Lenny had become a father to two beautiful young children and carried the responsibilities of husband and Dad with joy. My disappearing act had hurt him, and he subsequently sank into a period of depression. It was clear that Lenny still harboured feelings of resentment toward me. And he was happy to be talking again.

Our conversation hovered in the area of polite and friendly catching up for a while, but things took a turn at some point. Lenny started to vent some of his anger at me for making what he felt was a selfish choice to desert him and our family. Once he got started, he held nothing back.

I sat and listened as he vented anger and disappointment at me. The shift in our conversation happened so suddenly and with such little warning that I felt like a deer caught in headlights. I was stunned and frozen, unprepared for what was turning into a full-blooded verbal ass-kicking.

As Lenny's venting continued, it drifted into general attacks on my character. And as a result, I started getting angry, too.

I tried to reason with him that his words were becoming destructive, but my attempts at being a mediator were futile. Eventually, instead of trying to defend myself, I apologized and acknowledged the parts of what he was saying that I could admit were true. I had been selfish - I had made the selfish choice to disappear for years. He was right. I realized he was right about many things. His feelings, as uncomfortable as they were, made sense.

This concession helped calm things down, and by the time we finished our call, we were joking and talking in a calm, friendly way again.

When we got off the phone, however, I wondered if the conversation had been a disaster. Lenny's anger had been so intense it left me rattled.

I went outside for a walk to breathe some fresh air and clear my mind. As I calmed down, I discovered that one of my legs had gone numb and had a strange tingling sensation shooting up and down it. My whole body felt rocked by the intensity of what had just happened, and my numb/tingling leg seemed like a perfect manifestation of that. Maybe I just had my ass kicked so hard, on an emotional level, that it left my leg numb and buzzing.

The strength of Lenny's anger and resentment surprised me. I figured he would have been the easiest person in my family to talk to - but I had forgotten how fiery and passionate he could be (I had to laugh at myself for overlooking this part of my brother - it was a defining aspect of his personality, and probably one of his best qualities: His warrior spirit). I had also failed to realize how much Lenny cared about me and how much my rejection and disappearance had hurt him. As I wandered the streets of my neighbourhood with a limp, I let this reality sink in and wondered what the hell I had gotten myself into.

A few days later, I reached out to my older brother, Evan, with another brief, carefully worded email. Evan's response came quickly. In it, he shared that he had heard from Lenny about our recent conversation and was open to talking on the phone. After a few messages back and forth, we set up a time to chat, and I prepared for another difficult call.

When we got on the phone, there was initially a mountain of awkwardness and distance between us. Evan seemed to be at a loss for words, unsure of what to ask or share. The words he did speak were heavy with sadness and confusion - as though he had already mourned the loss of his brother years ago and didn't know quite how to interact with this person who was now re-appearing in his life.

As we talked, I apologized for my disappearance - for how I had cut myself out of his world. I described some of what had happened in my life over the years and asked him what had happened in his.

Like Lenny, he was married. He moved back to our hometown with his wife and got a job he liked, doing something he was passionate about. He had mellowed out, and his personality seemed to have softened with age. He sounded like he was doing great.

Between moments of awkwardness and discomfort, we stumbled into familiar territory: We talked about skateboarding (something we had both been obsessed with in our youth), rumours we heard about old long-lost friends, and music. A lot had changed over the years, but in some ways, nothing had.

Instead of being angry with me as Lenny had, Evan seemed more sad and removed. This dynamic made for a calmer conversation, and when we eventually got off the phone, I felt relieved.

As I reflected on the feelings of sadness, distance, and resentment that had resulted from my actions, I felt ready to take another step forward and reach out to my parents. By now, they would have heard through the grapevine that I was talking to my brothers and that it was only a matter of time before they heard from me.

When I saw that Mother's Day was approaching on the calendar, I thought it might be the perfect excuse to push past my resistance and take a leap. Then, the day arrived. I started my morning by heading to work for an unusually early and long shift. After a busy day serving families celebrating their mothers and grandmothers, I got home around ten o'clock in the evening and collapsed onto my bed in exhaustion. On the verge of falling asleep, I remembered that this was the day I was supposed to write my parents, and it was almost over. Under the pressure of limited time, I leapt up and into action. I opened my laptop and wrote a simple, sincere email to my Mom and Dad. I wished my Mom a happy Mother's Day and told both of them that I would love to talk sometime if they were open to that. I suspected that my Mom had almost certainly gone to bed before I hit send on that email, which made me feel a bit more embarrassed than I already would have been. Not only had I disappeared for years, but now I was returning, and I still couldn't remember Mother's Day.

The following morning, I woke up to a response from my parents. In it, they said they were excited to hear from me and would love to talk anytime. So, with a sickening nervousness in my gut, I picked up my phone and gave them a call.

My Mom answered. Initially, there was the same stilted awkwardness between us that I had felt with my brothers. After saying hello, my Mom had no idea where to begin - maybe it felt too raw and strange to be talking for any subject of conversation to make sense.

Realizing this, I tried to take the lead by sharing some of what had happened in my world over the years and why I had decided to reach out to them after so long. I expressed regret at what I had put them through. I apologized.

As we spoke, my Mom described something that my brothers had previously mentioned: She had already accepted years earlier that I was, in a sense, dead. I had vanished, and in such a sudden and complete way, for so long, that she had grieved the loss of her son - she let him go. Now, after she had mourned that death, I was back.

It was clear how relieved my mother was to finally be talking again. She was happy that I was no longer isolating myself and that she might have me back.

When she eventually passed the phone over to my Dad (who had been sitting beside her, occasionally adding his commentary in the background), he began by saying: "It doesn't matter what happened, Miles. We were hurt by what you chose. But we can't change that now. We love you, and we're happy you want to talk to us."

I was surprised to hear about the many things that had changed in my parents' world since I disappeared: My Mom had retired early from her job. In the years leading up to that, she had struggled with an autoimmune illness that she said had changed her perspective on life. They became grandparents. They also began travelling internationally and were eager to share stories from their adventures in faraway, exotic places. Ever the storyteller, my Dad got going on a tangent of assorted travel highlights as I sat and listened from a very different perspective than the last time we spoke.

One of my father's stories involved a trip he and my Mom had taken to Cambodia, where they stayed in a small village and volunteered with a local community organization. With great excitement, my Dad recounted the highlight of the trip: The days he spent volunteering in the village school, where he got to connect with children in their classroom.

"Oh, you wouldn't believe it, Miles," he explained. "Up in front of that class, I could just feel the love pouring out from all those little kids into me every day. Oh, it was unreal. That feeling was incredible - no words can describe it."

I sat in silent disbelief as my father continued sharing stories and observations. He talked about all the friends he had made during their travels. These were friends he met by simply being curious and talking to strangers. He talked about how that was always the best part of life: People and connection.

He spoke about my brothers and some of their challenges. He said the most important thing was that they did what made them happy - nothing else mattered.

As he spoke, my eyes widened, and I was overcome with astonishment - it felt like I was listening to myself talk. This man who valued love and connection sounded eerily like the man I thought I had been sculpting myself into. His words echoed the values I believed I had been learning about and discovering during the years when I had vanished from his world. I thought I had gone away and changed so much. I thought I had fashioned myself into an entirely new and different person. But my Dad sounded exactly like me. It freaked me out.

That conversation was the first of many over the following months. My wall was down now, and a door was open to my family. As we continued to speak, things gradually became less awkward. I learned more about what had happened in my parents' lives since I had been gone. And I also learned more about their past and who they were as people. I had a lot of questions now about my childhood and their childhoods - things that were a part of me which I did not quite understand.

The more I spoke with my father, the more I heard myself in his voice. This became a source of constant amazement to me. For years I developed a sense of pride in how different I had become from my family - how much work I had done on myself and how it had shaped me into something new. Now, speaking to my father after years of separation, I wondered if that sense of transformation was an illusion. I was no longer sure I had changed so much after all. And I couldn't tell if I had previously been seeing my father (or myself) clearly.

That September, I booked a week off from work and made plans to visit my parents for the first time in years.

I rented a car and drove several hours to my hometown during the first heavy fall rainstorm. As I drove along the familiar highway, every town I passed, every on-ramp, rest stop, and exit, was filled with memories and stories. I had hitchhiked along this highway countless times as a young traveller. I had tromped through many of the roadside forests bordering it and swam in many of the rivers it crossed. Because of this, everything I passed felt charged with history and personality. I felt affection and excitement as I drove by objects like telephone poles and blackberry patches I remembered. I noticed with admiration how much the trees on certain hillsides had grown. So much life had happened since I was last here, and I had forgotten how well I knew this land and how many stories unfolded in these places.

As I drove, I sat in silence, choosing to keep the car stereo turned off. Something was happening inside me that demanded attention: It felt like my body was changing energetically as I returned home - like it was letting everything in and re-tuning itself to the place it once knew very well. It felt like I was connecting to the past I tried for years to distance myself from and erase - to parts of my life (and myself) I had tried to forget. Coming back, letting myself feel these memories and this history, felt like it was doing something good inside me.

It was dark when I arrived at my parents' home. I pulled into their driveway and sat outside for a moment in the rental car, noticing the absolute quiet of their rural neighbourhood. I looked up at the house I lived in as a teenager, another place filled with memory and energy from my past - perhaps more than anywhere else.

I saw my parents peering out of the kitchen window at me and forced myself to leave the car, making my way to the front door. My Mom greeted me there, and we hugged each other. She was shorter than I remembered. Then my Dad and I hugged, and we proceeded to sit down together in the kitchen and catch up as they finished making dinner.

My parents looked older than I remembered (which they were). The hair on both their heads was white now - they had become grandparents and looked the part. I had also aged quite a bit - my head was shaved bald (in response to my thinning hair), and I had a short beard with accents of white throughout it. My skinny frame had more meat on it from the years of stable, consistent eating and time spent in the gym. I was no longer a boy - but maybe not a man yet.

We talked about the torrential rain I had been welcomed by on my drive (after months of sunny, bone-dry weather). We acknowledged how weird it was to be sitting in that kitchen together again after so long. I noticed how their house had changed through redecorations and renovations. There were photos of people I didn't recognize on their fridge - children, family members, and friends of theirs that I had never met or no longer recognized. There were simple drawings made by children hung on the walls - the artists behind these colourful images were their grandchildren (my niece and nephew), who I did not know.

When dinner was ready, my Dad poured each of us a glass of wine and offered a toast. His words were simple, and he fought back tears as he spoke them: "We love you, Miles. And we're so happy to have you here with us."

I found myself fighting back tears, too - though not entirely successfully.

After eating dinner and talking, I headed to bed for the night. I was surprised to learn that my parents had set up my old bedroom for me. This was the bedroom where I had spent my teenage years brooding in angst. It was the bedroom where I lost my virginity, discovered the power of literature, and dreamed of living a visionary, inspired life like the writers whose work I devoured.

At first, I thought sleeping in that room would be too weird - I feared regressing into an angsty teenage state. But as I opened the door and looked around, something about being there felt perfect.

The little single bed was exactly as I remembered - with the same corny, baseball-themed blanket covering it that I had used as a kid (despite never having any interest in baseball). I thought I had left no belongings behind at my parents' home, but it turned out that there were a few books on the shelf above the bed I must have forgotten about when I was getting rid of everything years earlier. I looked through this little collection - there were books by Krishnamurti, Hermann Hesse, and other authors I had been fascinated by in my youth.

There was one book on the shelf that I did not remember or recognize. It was titled: *The Noble Bloodlines*

Of Miles Olsen. On the inside cover was a note to me written by my second cousin, Perry. It read: "Merry Christmas 2014, Miles!"

I realized that this was a Christmas present I had never been around to receive. I knew my second cousin Perry was very interested in our family's history and had been compiling a detailed record of it. This book appeared to be the fruit of that labour. It was a large, thick text chronicling the history of my descendants, from my parents and grandparents to my Medieval ancestors.

Something about this book seemed hauntingly significant. Had I received it years earlier (when it was given to me), I would not have been interested in learning about my ancestry. But, at this moment, I found myself wildly fascinated by the souls who had come before me. I had returned to this home (and this bedroom) to reconcile with my origins. Finding a book here that reached far back into that story seemed very fitting.

Once I opened the book, I couldn't stop reading. I found stories about my great-grandparents getting married in downtown Vancouver a century ago - probably within a brief walk of the apartment where I lived. I imagined the love they might have felt, their excitement, personalities, and struggles. I devoured little glimpses into the worlds of my dead forebears with fascination until I realized several hours had passed, and I had better try to get some rest.

I turned the lights off and climbed into bed, but sleep seemed impossible. As I lay awake in the dark, something strange overcame me. There was a buzzing energy throughout my body - a sense of movement or vibration unlike anything I had felt before. I was wide awake but seemingly in an altered state of consciousness. Gradually, the sensations grew until I had the distinct impression that something was being rewritten in me. Something I had been carrying internally for a long time was transforming, changing, reorganizing - receiving an update. After years of separation and life, I had returned to this place, and simply laying my body to rest here was doing something profound to it. It felt like I was recalibrating. And it was not a willful thing - not something I was doing, but something happening automatically.

Given the book I had just been poring over, I wondered if these feelings were somehow related to the spirit of my ancestors. It felt like I had opened myself up to a force I had been closed off from for years: The energy of my roots and origins.

For a long time, I wanted nothing to do with my past or the people I came from. But now I was here, curious and open, and I felt a current of energy and love rushing through me as though it had been waiting for me to return to this place and drop my guard. It was intense, uncomfortable, weird, and beautiful. For a long time, I lay in the dark, motionless, with this energy surging powerfully through my body. It felt good - like taking potent drugs that helped me process old emotions and let something new in.

I won't pretend to understand what I was experiencing that night. But it was the beginning of a feeling that would follow me for months afterwards - a feeling of connection to those I come from. A feeling that they are part of me, that they are with me, and that this is a source of strength.

During my visit, I spent an afternoon alone with my older brother, Evan. Being around him felt easy and natural - the awkwardness and distance that had been between us on the phone fell apart more gracefully in person.

I could see how he had matured and grown over the years. He was an incredibly committed husband and loved the people he was close to. There were moments when I could feel a sense of judgement or condescension from him regarding my choices over the years, but I couldn't blame him for that. I even agreed with most of his discernments. And the tender part of me that might have felt affected and hurt by such judgement in the past wasn't bothered. I could see how, from his perspective, I'd kind of gone crazy. And I was okay with that. I could also feel how much he appreciated me.

For most of my visit home, I did very little. I went for morning walks in the forest near my parents' house, talked with them about life, and visited my old stomping grounds. I walked the banks of local rivers and watched the fall salmon run, then wandered neighbourhoods and forested areas filled with memories, surprised by how they had changed.

On the last day of my visit, I drove an hour south along the highway to visit Lenny for the first time since I disappeared. We had arranged to connect briefly in the afternoon when he got off work. Lenny and I hadn't been speaking much, as he wanted very little to do with me after a couple of initial conversations on the phone. When planning this visit, I asked if he wanted to get together, and he reluctantly squeezed me into a brief moment of his schedule. As the working father of two young children, he was busy. But while I prepared to see him for the first time in years, I got the sense it was more than just busyness that made him seem so preoccupied and limited with his availability.

We met in the parking lot of a strip mall near his work, and I suggested we grab something to eat. After finding a Vietnamese restaurant and sitting down together, we began to talk about life. I can't remember much of our conversation - only that Lenny felt aloof, distant, and almost a bit hostile toward me. There were moments when he spoke with judgment and condescension about the details of my life that were hard to stomach. But I did my best to take it all lightly, holding my pride and anger back, as I was not there to fuel tensions further.

Lenny made it through his bowl of soup faster than me, and as soon as I finished mine, he seemed ready to carry on with his afternoon and say goodbye. We hugged each other, then he jumped into his truck and peeled out of the parking lot.

For a while, I sat in that parking lot, sad. This person I once knew so well was now a distant stranger. Our lives did not touch - there was a wall between us and no indication of that changing.

As I drove back to my parents' house feeling this sadness, I thought: Maybe that was the first tiny step towards rebuilding something. This may take time - it may take lots and lots of time. I guess that's fair.

When we first reconnected on the phone, Lenny told me that he had lost his trust in me and feared I would just disappear again if he let me back into his life. Given that loss of trust, I knew I might need some patience with his process. I would need to earn that trust back.

As I drove in silence, reflecting on these things, I accepted that this was a consequence of my actions. I had hurt my brother, and now I had to bear the awkward discomfort of facing that. I had to give him the grace to feel mad at me for as long as he needed. I had to calm my pride and ego, which was no small task.

In the space that had grown between us, I struggled to do one of the most challenging and obvious things: To give him understanding, patience, and acceptance. I knew I would be a coward and a hypocrite if I did anything less.

By the end of my visit, I felt ready to head home and return to everyday life. As I said goodbye to my parents,

I felt deep gratitude for these two people who had raised me, put up with my wanderings, and accepted me back into their world after I rejected them and vanished for so long.

I had a lot to think about in the wake of this trip. On the surface, very little had happened. But on a deeper level, something enormous transpired. I had returned to my home and family, and everything looked very different. Maybe because I had severed myself from that world so completely, I was forced to become an emotionally autonomous person in a way that was quite healthy. And because of that separation, when I returned, I did not go back as a child who wanted his parents to take care of him, to be perfect, spotless beings, or anything other than who they were. When they did little things that would have previously driven me up the wall, made me erupt into a volcano of frustration, or feel a sense of rejection, I watched with wonder. I wasn't numb emotionally, and I did get triggered here and there, but it was different. I wasn't waiting for them to take care of me or to change.

Those years of isolation and disconnection had made for a very awkward return, but something good had come out of them. I could see my family, and my parents in particular, as people. I could see them with reverence. And I could also see that I was a composition of them, a blend of them. I carried their gifts and their burdens. And after years of obsessing over their (and my) burdens, it was fascinating to see how much more significant their gifts felt now.

Over the following months, I marvelled at how taking down a wall inside me and reconnecting to my family felt like letting a basic form of love back into my life. It echoed through my body, mind, and world - it was a powerful force to let in.

When I first chose to reconnect with my family, I assumed that I had become a wise, intelligent person who could bring understanding and healing to them. But as I waded through the messy, awkward reality, the opposite seemed more accurate: I had returned with a gaping hole in me that was filled up by the simple, unpretentious truth of the people and place I came from. I did not return to bring wisdom or heal others - I returned to receive something I didn't know I was missing.

Seven

Nine months after my first visit back home, I returned with a box of books and my friend, Pandora. My new book had been published for a year and a half, but because of rapidly changing restrictions on gatherings, I had yet to do a single public event to support its release. With the easing of regulations starting to appear more stable and reliable, I decided to plan a series of belated book launch events over the summer. As I considered where to hold the first of these events, I felt that returning to my hometown would be a fitting place to begin.

Finding an available venue there was surprisingly challenging. This may have been because events had not happened for the past two years. After some persistence, I found a space to rent for an evening. Once that was secured, I contacted local newspapers with a press release and did whatever else I could to spread the word about my book launch. I invited Pandora to join me on this trip because it would be fun to have a friend around, and I could also use her help practically with setting things up.

On the day of the event, we drove several hours in the warm June sun, occasionally stopping at lookout points and beaches to stare at the ocean, breathe in the seaside air, and enjoy the late-spring scenery. We arrived at the venue early, with plenty of time to eat snacks, arrange rows of chairs, and set up the PA system I had rented. Once we finished setting everything up, it was time to wait.

I had no idea how many people to expect. The last time I did something like this (when my first book was published ten years earlier), I was surprised by the crowd that assembled. But this was a different time. I had been gone from this town for years and lost contact with most of the people I had known here. I was hopeful there would be a decent turnout - but I braced for the possibility that nobody would show up besides my parents and one or two close friends.

As the start time approached, people began to arrive. The first person to show up was a ninety-year-old woman who walked into the hall and told me we had met a decade earlier at a craft fair, where I sold her a copy of my first book. Then another stranger arrived, who I warmly welcomed and introduced myself to. Shortly after, another young woman I had never met walked into the hall.

Gradually, more people trickled in, and I welcomed many of them individually and exchanged a few words before they found a place to sit. I noticed that I had grown much more comfortable doing this in the years since I last played the role of a public-facing author. I suspected that being a waiter had taught me something about hospitality and strengthened my ability to comfortably push through awkwardness, say hello, and be kind to strangers.

There might have been twenty people in attendance by the time my talk began - I was too nervous and focused on the task at hand to notice such details with any clarity. These were mostly people I did not know, with a few old friends and familiar faces thrown into the mix.

I had many brief interactions with kind people after finishing my talk. But one exchange, in particular, left an impression on me. A young man who had looked very engaged and intense during my presentation came and shook my hand firmly before asking a pointed question: "Miles, you mentioned during your talk the years you spent living in the woods, close to the land. Now that you live in a city, you must still get out into real wild nature often, right? I mean, after the amount of time you spent on the land, I feel like you would *have* to. You *have* to escape all that noise and feel the openness, right?"

He was referring to a part of my talk where I briefly mentioned my years living in backwoods cabins I built with friends. It was a chapter of my life I only touched on in passing, but it piqued his curiosity.

I answered him honestly: "I barely get out of the city. I walk in the forest near my house every day, and it feels like probably the most important part of my life. But getting out and into the kind of real wild nature you're talking about - oh man, it doesn't happen enough. I definitely should leave the city and get out there. During my years living in the woods, life felt so luxurious. But that was a long time ago - it feels like a distant fantasy now. All that silence and stillness, the magic of nature, it feels like another world, another life."

He stared into my eyes and said: "Miles, *you need to get out there*. I mean this, man. *You have to*. Promise me you'll take yourself somewhere quiet and feel how good it is. You need that in your life, brother. Believe me."

His voice was filled with gravity and concern - like he knew something I didn't. Maybe he knew how serious this was. As we shook hands and said goodbye, I was surprised by how much I was letting his words in. Typically, when people came to me with unsolicited advice, I would ignore it. But he had been so well-intentioned, sincere, and worried - I wondered if he was onto something.

Pandora and I stayed with my parents for a couple of days after the book-launch event, visiting with them and some old friends in the area. On our last night there, we had dinner with my parents. After eating and talking around the kitchen table, I decided to walk down to the ocean. Pandora joined me, and we made our way to the beach in the warm June evening.

When we got to the water, we sat down on the pebble surface of the beach and leaned against a big old driftwood log. A cluster of wild rose bushes was flowering nearby, and the air was filled with the rich scent of their blossoms, along with the sweet aromatic fragrance of fresh green foliage bursting open on all the surrounding trees and plants. The combination of all these scents was intoxicating - it smelled like we were in a heavenly garden.

The moment we sat on that beach, I was struck by the ocean's stillness. It appeared motionless, reflecting the gorgeous cloud patterns of the fading dusk sky like a mirror. I was also moved by this scene's utter silence and uninterrupted wildness. No houses, streetlamps, or human-made buildings were visible in any direction. A few boys were struggling to set up a tent at the far end of the beach - aside from that, there was nothing but nature and silence. No faraway hum of roadways or machinery. Just pure, beautiful silence.

Looking at the sky and its reflection on the water, I thought: THIS IS WHAT HEAVEN LOOKS LIKE. I couldn't imagine any heaven, any celestial realm, looking more like heaven than the scene before me. The play of light, emptiness, and cloud in the sky - the feeling of perfect stillness in the ocean and the mountain range lurking behind it in the distance, seemed like a divine vision. As I soaked in this earth-heaven scene, something interesting happened.

As I continued to stare at the sky, it felt like the beauty I was looking at was pouring into me. It felt like a drug - an altered state of consciousness - stretching me open, filling me with the energy of this heaven, and the longer I looked, the higher I got. It was wildly exhilarating, and there was something scary about how intense and out of the ordinary it was. Even maintaining my gaze on the sky began to feel painful - the energy pouring into me was so much, so beautiful, it was hard to bear.

"Pandora," I said, with my eyes fixed on the clouds, "are you feeling this?"

"I feel high," she responded. "It's like I'm on crazy drugs."

"Yeah, me too. Holy shit, THIS IS INSANE. The longer you look at the sky, *the more it comes into you.*"

We sat, transfixed, for a long time. Occasionally, we would try to describe what we were feeling, and as strange as it should have sounded, we knew exactly what the other was talking about. We had stumbled into a mutually shared spontaneous natural high, an ecstatic altered state, provoked perhaps by just sitting at the right spot, on the right night, near some special wild rose bushes.

As we continued sitting there, I felt waves of euphoria. My heart filled with a glowing, almost painful sensation. I began to feel a sense of connection to the energy of the earth itself - whatever that means. And as that earth energy filled me, it felt like I was instantly incredibly rich. The exact thought that flashed into my awareness was: *I feel like a king.*

I realized that this was something I had felt before - I remembered it from my youth - I remembered this exact feeling from my years living on the land: *This was the feeling of being connected to nature.* There was a sense of being lifted, or supercharged, by the energy of the land -

a sense of being filled with spiritual affluence or a vast, energetic wealth that resulted from being connected to this living world.

I suddenly recalled how confident, exuberant, and blessed I had felt during that long-ago chapter of life. Normally, when I looked back at the confidence I felt during those youthful years, I thought it was simply a result of my young, untempered male ego. But I was now catching a glimpse of another factor - one I had forgotten about and maybe never appreciated: From where I was sitting, it looked like the exuberant sense of confidence I felt during my years living close to the land was a result of being connected to this energy. I had felt like a king back then - I had believed in myself with reckless abandon because I was filled with the spirit of the land. There was something bigger than me that perfumed my life, that I let into my heart - and it gave me a gift. It was not entirely *me* that had been so confident - it was something powerful that I had infused myself with. It was the pure, unadulterated drug I binged on: Nature.

As Pandora and I sat, churning through transcendent, altered states of consciousness, I said: "We have to remember this. We have to come back to these quiet places often. This is where we lived when we were younger. That's why we were happy and confident. We didn't give a shit about what anybody thought of us because we were connected to *this*."

As the last light of dusk faded and the sky slowly went dark, we both returned to a somewhat normal state of consciousness, in awe of what we had just experienced. The more we spoke about it, the more it seemed like we had just gone through the same thing.

We sat talking in the dark for a while. During our conversation, I remembered the intense young man I spoke to after my book event a few nights earlier.

"He told me I need to connect to nature," I shared. "And he said it with this concern and compassion that was incredibly touching - like he was really worried about me. I think this is what he was talking about. And he was right - I feel like we were just touched by something I've been starved of for years. This might be why I came here this weekend - to have that conversation and sit on this beach. To be reminded of a power I forgot."

After a moment of silence, Pandora responded: "That sounds about right."

When we returned to the city, I found that the reality of my life there had become almost unbearable. After just a taste of movement in my life as an author, and the expanded state of consciousness Pandora and I had touched that night on the beach, what had previously been an enjoyable, day-to-day existence, suddenly felt dead.

On my first day back at work, I felt a horrifying heaviness. My coworkers seemed depressed and cynical. The people I served were immature, entitled, and petty. I had just touched another life - I just had a glimpse of being an author in the real world and a taste of the power of nature. In the wake of that, returning to the humdrum reality of working as a waiter in the city felt crushing.

My newfound bitterness caught me by surprise. Over days and weeks, I watched myself become progressively more negative at work. I felt overcome by feelings of resentment, apathy, and restlessness. And it slowly dawned on me that I might have no choice but to quit my job - partly because it felt unfair to everyone around me to be so miserable and negative. I was becoming something I didn't want to be.

One day after a shift, I confided in my coworker, Dee: "I've been so happy here these past few years," I explained. "People aren't supposed to be this happy at a dead-end job - I've really been irrationally content."

"I know," he responded, "it's weird."

"Yeah, but it's over," I continued. "My spark is gone. I feel totally over it. I feel burned out - like I got a taste of another chapter of life, and I can't bear being here anymore."

"I get it, brother," Dee said. "Don't leave, though. Please, don't leave me here!"

Dee was joking, though I appreciated the sentiment. He understood why I was on the verge of quitting, and for a moment, it seemed like the only rational choice.

However, as the weeks passed and I soberly considered my options, my humility gradually returned. After many conversations with friends and coworkers, I realized I wasn't ready to move on. My restlessness and desire to impulsively quit my job after a taste of another life didn't feel grounded or mindful.

As an author, I was making very little money. If I factored in the amount of time, energy, and resources I poured into that part of my life, it was not a job - it was a strange obsession. Making it into a livelihood would take time, dedication, ingenuity, and possibly some serious luck or divine help. Having a stable, simple job working with people I loved that gave me plenty of free time and flexibility to write seemed incredibly wise.

So as much as I had been tempted to throw a grenade into my stable, comfortable life - to shake things up and force myself into something new and unfamiliar, I talked myself out of it. It seemed that the challenge at this moment was to *not* throw a bomb into my life. To not quit my job - but instead, to look at the big picture, put my head down, and work.

After a few weeks passed, I came down from the high of my time away. The infusion of energy I had received from giving a talk to an audience of real people wore off, as did the powerful surge of nourishment I had received from nature. I adjusted back to my life.

One day during a slow shift at the restaurant, a coworker asked me about my thoughts on psychedelics. She was shocked to learn that I had no experience with them and had not used any mind-altering substances (besides caffeine and an occasional alcoholic beverage) for many years. She told me how amazing mushrooms and other hallucinogens were, how much they had changed her life, and how I needed to explore them.

I explained to her that I didn't feel like I needed any drugs - I felt like I had already gone to some of the places they take people. They seemed helpful to others, but I was convinced I didn't require them, and they weren't for me.

Our conversation had an argumentative tone, and I walked away from it feeling surprised at myself. By the end of it, I had become emotionally charged and defensive, and I was pretty sure I had just acted like a closed-minded, insecure, arrogant man. It seemed true that, for a long time, I benefitted from living a drug and substance-free life. But I couldn't deny what just happened: I had played the role of a guy who doesn't know anything about the matter at hand yet has allowed himself to form a rigid opinion from his place of ignorance.

For the rest of my shift, I reflected on that brief interaction. I felt the residue of defensiveness and pride it had provoked in me, and I arrived at a sobering realization: *I think I was wrong. I didn't know what I was talking about, and instead of admitting that, I was arrogant.*

I humbly confessed this to my coworker before the night was through, but the impact of our interaction didn't stop there. As I reflected on my rigidity and closed-mindedness, I realized that I should probably try taking mushrooms - in fact, it felt like I needed to. Not because I particularly wanted to get high on them - but because I didn't want to be a closed-minded, arrogant man blinded by his limited experiences. I wanted to challenge my assumptions and my pride. When or how I would go about this wasn't clear, but I knew I would have to do it at some point.

A few weeks later, Pandora gave me a very unusual birthday present: A microdose of psilocybin mushrooms. We had never spoken about hallucinogens before - except for me to say that I had no interest in them. Given this, the timing of her gift was remarkable, and I accepted it with gratitude and an open mind. She shared how it seemed like mushrooms could help me and that it had felt important for her to offer them to me as a gift at this moment.

A few days later, I had an evening off from work with no plans, so I decided to take the small dose of dried mushrooms Pandora gave me. I ate them in the early evening in my apartment and then decided to take a walk in the forest and watch the sunset as they kicked in. Pandora had explained that it might take an hour for me to feel any effects, and that the amount she had given me was so small most people would not notice any shift in their conscious awareness (but I might). With this in mind, I waited nearly an hour after eating them before heading out into the world.

As I left my apartment and walked toward the park, I immediately noticed a shift in my awareness: The brick sidewalk, and the way the evening sunlight splashed across it, had a striking, almost monumental beauty. I felt absorbed in it, touched by it. I thought to myself: *I'm noticing beauty differently. Cool.*

When I got to the park, my first destination was a pond populated by countless ducks. Walking along the edge of the water, I noticed the ducks differently than usual: I could see how unbelievably *open* the ducks were. They had a complete lack of self-consciousness - a pure, wild, natural nakedness. I was absorbed by it - it touched me.

Then, as I continued, I noticed a similar, albeit less intense version of that raw openness in the blackberry vines lining the forest path I walked along. It was beautiful.

As people walked past me, I felt something that seemed like the exact opposite of that openness: I was painfully aware of their pretensions, their dishonesty, their masks, and their egos. Being around their jumbled personas was so uncomfortable that I had to avert my eyes. I needed boundaries so strong that even looking at them was too intimate.

This sense of revulsion bothered me. I was used to seeing the complexity of people - the twists and turns of their personalities - and finding the beauty within them. I had trained myself to look for the sacred in others. And on this tiny dose of mushrooms, I found myself simply repulsed by it all. I wasn't sure if I liked that.

After a long, meditative walk, I went home that night fascinated by this subtle experience. I still wasn't sure if I liked it, but I was certain I needed to experience more - I was too curious now.

Over the following months, I took increasingly larger doses of mushrooms and found myself fascinated by what I discovered. The most impactful of these experiences happened near the end of the summer.

By now, I was becoming more excited about mushrooms. The glimpses of altered perception and ecstatic openness I had experienced while on them felt like they were re-awakening a part of my spirit. After one of my doses, I felt a residual vitality, courage, and passion for life that carried through the drudgery of everyday existence for weeks like an enduring gift. My experimentation was opening and refreshing my thinking in very healthy ways. I was growing respect and admiration for these mushrooms as a powerful emotional and spiritual tool, albeit one that I still did not understand well. My previous closed-minded assumptions were falling apart, and I was happy about that.

I approached this experimentation with humility, generally leaving a month or more between doses to fully return to my grounded, stable mental reality. The unpredictable, destabilizing nature of mushrooms seemed to require my being in a very solid place psychologically. There were many times when I thought I wanted to take a dose, but my gut told me *no* - I was not grounded or emotionally stable enough, and because of that, it felt like I would have a negative experience.

In the spirit of this enthusiasm and humility, I took my largest dose yet of dried mushrooms (which was still relatively moderate) on a sunny afternoon.

After eating them, I took a shower, washed some dishes, and left my apartment - heading for the natural beauty of the forest nearby. This time, as I started to feel the effects of the mushrooms, it was not subtle. I could feel my consciousness get hit by waves of disorientation - being stretched, pulled, sped up, and slowed down. I felt pangs of intense nausea and panic, which I combatted with deep, abdominal breathing. With each step that my awareness took away from ordinary consciousness, I felt a primal fear in me being triggered.

This fear seemed like it could instantly turn an experience into a bad trip if I allowed myself to run with it. So, as my perception of time and space started to blur - as my visual perception began taking on a strange, distorted hue - I watched the compensatory pangs of fear that started screaming through me carefully.

When I was younger, this kind of fear would have seized and possessed me completely. But after years of isolation and inner work, I felt like this fear was an old friend - a part of me I knew pretty well and that I treated not all that differently from my nausea: I breathed into my belly and tried my best not to focus on it. Focusing on the fearful voice made it feel more scary and real - it made the fear grow.

So I focused on the trees. I focused on the reality of my environment. I focused on my breath. I remembered that fear naturally appears at the threshold of a new awareness. And then, to my relief, there would be moments of peace and calm.

As I walked deeper into the forest, many waves of nausea and fear passed, each seeming to mark a further stretch away from ordinary waking consciousness. Gradually, I started to realize: *I am really fucking high.* A part of me wanted to go home, to be safe and contained in the fortress of my apartment - not alone in this big forest with creepy men and wild animals. But something pushed me to keep walking deeper, knowing I needed to be among the trees. My fear could wait for another day to hide.

As I continued walking further into the forest, something in the lower corner of my vision caught my attention: The skin on my hands, dangling below my waist as I walked, was dark brown. As I looked down at my hands and noticed this strange glitch in reality, I was overcome with the sensation of being a woman - an older woman. I could feel her emotional disposition - she was fiery, strong, maternal, and a bit distrustful of life. She had dark skin and a voluptuous mother's body. At that moment, I only felt her feelings, thoughts, and way of living and breathing. My hips swayed like her hips as I walked. Miles felt like a distant memory, an unfamiliar persona. I was now this woman.

While this was happening, I remembered an experience I had years earlier: In the wake of Kevin's death, I became fascinated by concepts of reincarnation and past lives. At one point, I played with a method of past-life regression using a guided meditation. During that meditation, I briefly witnessed a scene in my mind's eye. In it, a black woman was lying dead beside a car, and it looked like she had been shot - blood had pooled onto the concrete beside her. A couple of bystanders watched helplessly as I hovered over the drama, unsure of what I was looking at.

I never thought anything of that experience and figured it was probably just my imagination conjuring something up to fill in the space of the meditation. It certainly didn't register as a past life that I was peeking into - just something curious that appeared in my mind.

But now, it felt like I *was* that woman. I felt like I knew her better than I knew Miles. I felt her strong personality and the burden of her life's oppressions - the injustice of living life as a black woman and a mother who had to defend herself from a world that did not treat her with respect or dignity. I felt her reality buzzing through me - like something I had been carrying my whole life - a pain buried inside me, now moving.

And then, as though I was watching a distant story unfold, I saw how strange an opportunity it was for her to continue her journey as a soul in the body of Miles: A white man. A man who might look exactly like the people who had caused her the most hardship throughout her life. A man born into privilege simply due to the container of his body - in direct contrast to her experience.

I did not feel more affinity with either her or Miles - I was simply observing everything with a certain degree of awe, a sense of being removed while feeling the residue of her emotions and experiences wash through me. It seemed as though something was processing or metabolizing - feelings frozen in time were thawing and moving without any conscious understanding or effort on my part. I continued walking further into the forest.

Then, as quickly as that woman's consciousness had overtaken me, it was gone. I snapped back into the present moment in the forest - aware of the towering trees, mosses, and ferns around me and their extraordinary aliveness. A small path broke away from the main trail I was on, and something told me to go up it. The moment I did, a massive, moss-enshrouded maple tree revealed itself in the distance at the centre of a meadow.

This maple appeared to have started its life growing on top of a rotting tree trunk, which had completely disintegrated and disappeared over time. Now, it was suspended in the air, six feet high, by a tangle of thick roots that held it above the forest floor. The tangled, interwoven tree roots that propped it above the ground contained a hollow, cave-like center where there used to be a large rotting tree trunk. This space was big enough to fit several people inside it.

I stood in awe of this magnificent tree and the womb-like root structure it rested upon. In my altered state of consciousness, I felt that I was in the presence of a goddess - a grandmother of the forest - and that I must conduct myself with the utmost integrity while in her presence. I slowly walked across the meadow towards her, my head bowed in reverence, knowing that I was in the company of a divine being. For a while, I stood and stared in silence. I felt the power of this tree - I felt like it knew all of the secrets of creation. I looked into the hollow space at its core - the room crafted from its tangled roots. And in the walls of that room, I saw the faces of souls. I saw fear, pain, cowardice, jealousy, ugliness, and joy - all of the faces of humanity - and it was overwhelming.

Eventually, I moved further away from the trail and into the forest. I saw a young Douglas fir tree, and something told me to go and touch it. I walked up to it and hesitated, afraid someone might stumble across me hugging this tree and think I looked weird.

Then, a voice inside me said: "Miles, you do not have a choice here. *Do not be a coward!* This moment is what life is for. Your hesitation is your fear of intimacy, and you can't hide anymore. TOUCH THAT TREE! DO YOU HEAR ME? DO NOT HIDE FROM THIS INTIMACY."

I took a breath, let go of my fear and embarrassment, and put both of my hands on the trunk of that fir tree. I stared at its mossy, furrowed bark and suddenly felt like I was staring into a lover's eyes. I felt a wave of euphoria pour through me, and my jaw dropped as I experienced the kind of ecstatic intimacy and union I had only ever felt with a woman.

I giggled, barely believing what was happening, and held on to that tree. Without any movement - without anything sexual transpiring - it felt like we were making love. It felt unbelievably pure, intimate, and sacred. When I finally let go, I looked around myself - there were a lot of other trees that looked like I should touch them. So that's what I did. I slowly made my way around the forest, occasionally stopping to hold a tree - feeling a different kind of chemistry, energy, and personality with each of them.

I sat at the foot of that big, hollow grandmother maple tree for a while and stared at the moss on a rotting log beside me in wonderment.

"This is it," I thought. "This is what I've been missing. I lost my connection to the earth. I lost the best thing ever. I lost a part of myself."

As I strung these thoughts together, it was as though I could hear another voice laughing at me. At the time, I thought this was the consciousness of the mushrooms themselves lovingly mocking me, saying: *"This is the most obvious thing ever. Of course, he comes full circle and returns to find himself in nature. Who could have seen it coming? Hahahaha!"*

It was getting dark now, and I knew that although I wanted to stay and play in the forest longer, I needed to get home and get warm. On my walk back, I was stopped repeatedly by enormous, ancient, Western Red Cedar trees along my path. I felt their energy and personality, and could hear what they were thinking. These giants of the forest felt like gorgeous, voluptuous, wise older women. The smooth, longitudinal striations of their bark were like the natural curves of a woman's body, and I stared at them, enveloped by their beauty. I felt like a young stud that these sensual, mature women were checking out - I could feel their affection and excitement toward me. I stood and stared at them in awe. I touched their massive trunks, mesmerized that I shared a world with these monumental, divine life forms. It felt like we were flirting telepathically - and also like I needed to get home before it got completely dark, which I told them as I scurried along the path.

Seven

"Sorry ladies, gotta go!"

In the aftermath of that experience, I found a part of myself blown open that had been closed for ages: An intimate, spiritual love for nature that was at the centre of my life once upon a time. In my zealous pursuit of healing or growth, I had severed my connection to that source of sustenance. When I left my old cabin in the woods years earlier and became, to borrow Thoreau's phrase, a sojourner in the civilized world, a relationship ended. I turned my back on something which, up to that point, had been the focus of my life. And to be honest, I never gave that course of action a second thought. I moved on - there were new adventures before me, new mysteries to explore, and I simply considered that chapter of my life over. But after my experience in the forest that day, I knew I had been missing something.

Over the following weeks, my morning walks began to take a very different form. Where before, I had gone on roughly the same walk every day and enjoyed my time in nature in a very relaxed, calm state, there was now a sense of heightened passion and intimacy with the forest. My walks became much longer. I wandered off the trails and explored new routes into different parts of the forest, stunned by the beauty and spirit of the life around me. I was paying closer attention. It felt like being in love.

During the peak of my mushroom trip in the woods, I stumbled upon what I thought at the time was a wild mushroom I recognized: A northwestern Reishi - a local variant of a mushroom prized in traditional Chinese medicine for a host of powerful healing properties. When I discovered this mushroom during the peak of my high, I almost lost my mind with excitement. It seemed that one mushroom had guided me to another, and I was meant to learn about this beautiful fungus growing near where I lived.

So, on a morning walk shortly after that trip, I returned to the old, dead hemlock tree where I believed I had discovered that Reishi mushroom growing. When I got there, I was happy to find that there was indeed a mushroom that looked exactly how I remembered the Reishi - and several more gorgeous specimens were fruiting on the trunk of this dead, decaying tree. I was just as excited to see these mushrooms now, completely sober, as I had been when I was high. They were physically stunning: A deep, crimson-red colour with a glossy, reflective surface that glistened in the dim rainforest light. To me, they seemed powerful, intelligent, and sacred.

The thought of harvesting one of them to brew into a tea occurred to me (in fact, there was a part of me that felt like I *needed* to do this), but I was happy to simply witness their beauty. I was still unsure if I knew how to identify these mushrooms correctly, and I was not comfortable harvesting them without knowing how abundant they were in the area and having a sense of what kind of impact that might have. So I left those beautiful Reishi mushrooms alone.

Then, to my surprise, I began to find them growing elsewhere. As I continued exploring deeper into the forest during my daily walks, I discovered numerous dead, decaying trees with plenty of stunning specimens of these special mushrooms fruiting on them. After some research, I grew more confident with my identification (though still not certain), and my morning walks became consumed by my over-enthusiastic mushroom discoveries.

I was not harvesting any of the mushrooms I found - I was just observing them in awe. Something about their mere existence and form amazed me - the unique shape, size, and character that each mushroom had, and the nature of their existence living on dead bodies (in this case, dead trees), part of a matrix of mycelium travelling through darkness, earth, and decaying matter to emerge in this stunning incarnation. There was something strangely mystical about their existence. They were a kind of intermediary between the living and the dead - a gatekeeper or facilitator of life's transformation from one body to another.

My fascination with these mushrooms took me into parts of the forest I would not have visited otherwise. During a walk, I would glimpse a decaying tree trunk in the distance and make my way there to see if it had mushrooms growing on it. This led me to gorgeous meadows and stunning Tolkienesque fantasy landscapes.

I would often sit down and soak in the beauty of these pockets of forest, breathing in the air, feeling the stable, supportive nature of the strong, silent trees around me - grateful to be alive, grateful to be on earth, grateful to be back in connection with the land.

One day, I checked in on some of the Reishi mushrooms I had been watching grow over the past several weeks and was shocked to discover that someone had come and harvested all of them. With sadness in my heart, I went to look at another patch of these mushrooms I had been keeping my eyes on and discovered that they, too, had been picked clean. Not one of them was left. My gut sank.

I marched through the forest, stopping by each of the many spots where I had discovered these mushrooms growing. Every one of them had been stripped bare - all of the mushrooms were gone.

Eventually, I sat down on a log that had fallen across the forest floor and felt a mixture of sadness and anger. I felt angry at the greed and stupidity of humans, who see something beautiful and take every last piece of it. It made me sick.

Then, I felt stupid for not having the guts to harvest a single one of those mushrooms myself. I had just stared at them - feeling like I didn't want to harm them, feeling that I probably wasn't worthy of taking anything from such beauty. It was too sacred - I didn't want to mess it up.

In the end, someone with more entitlement and gusto than me came along and claimed all of it for themselves. My tiptoeing and restraint had been pointless.

As I kicked myself, I also knew I would not change how I had chosen to behave. In a sense, it was more beautiful to simply witness those mushrooms - to study and become close to them. And maybe that person was also right to go ahead and harvest them. It may have made no difference ecologically - they were prolific in those woods, and many mushrooms remained out of sight and out of reach, spreading spores and reproducing.

After wandering broken-hearted through the forest for a day, I decided to challenge my sense of sadness and frustration: I would walk deeper into the woods and find out if there were, in fact, plenty more of these mushrooms that the mysterious harvester had not found or gotten their hands on.

With this mission in mind, my morning walks drew me into unfamiliar parts of the forest, where to my surprise and delight, I found many old, dead trees colonized by shiny, crimson-red Reishi mushrooms. Led by my searching into quiet stands of cedar and hemlock, I was touched by the beauty that surrounded me. It was as though my fascination with these mushrooms had been a tool - a way of pulling me further into the forest and the quiet, sacred places I would not have stumbled into otherwise. These were special places, and it felt like a gift to have been pulled to them.

In this state of fascination, my morning walks stretched longer and longer. I headed into the woods with the passion and openness of a man who'd fallen in love with someone and wanted to surround himself with their energy. There was an electricity, excitement, and reverence at every new thing I noticed or learned about this place. On these walks, it felt almost as though I was still high on psychoactive mushrooms - but maybe now I was just high from the land.

I had been walking through these woods every morning for years, yet now something was completely different. There was an extreme openness in me. When I found myself in the silent, misty, moss-enshrouded reaches of the forest, there was a sense of humility at the sanctity before me. There was a respect for the earth. A feeling of being very small, very young, and very naive in relation to the wisdom of the place I was standing. A sense of bowing down and being held by something much greater than me - a higher power. And this higher power was not abstract - it did not require any faith or belief. No, this was a higher power that surrounded me, that I could see with my eyes and touch with my hands. Through the energy of those trees and all the living things surrounding them, I felt an immense sense of strength and a deep understanding of my insignificance and fragility.

I had no idea how I lived without this (or how anyone does). I became so neurotic, aimless, and confused without a connection to the earth - without being brought back to reality by touching something much bigger than myself.

As I felt the significance of this reconnection, a strange sadness overcame me, a kind of grief. I grieved that, for nearly a decade, I had turned my back on this love. In my youth, I fed my relationship to nature gratuitously. I lived in hand-built cabins for years, surrounded by the natural world I worshipped. The emotional nourishment I received from that was monumental: I lived in the hands of my God. I engaged in an ongoing, direct relationship with that God - touching it, breathing it in, studying it, and learning from its rhythms.

And then, I walked away. A new chapter arrived. I realized that living close to nature had been, in some ways, a hiding place - a way of avoiding the world, my challenges, and the difficulty of human relationships. And so I cut myself off from it. I turned towards a new focus and left that relationship behind.

Now, it appeared to have been a perfect love that I abandoned. I felt the kind of remorse I would expect a man to feel years after divorcing the love of his life and having a moment of truth - a sober realization of the unconditional love he took for granted and turned his back on. At that moment, he might recognize that he once had everything, and he threw it away because of his restlessness and lack of understanding.

I felt this sadness (and even anger) at my choices as I went on my morning walks in the woods. There was a sense that the land didn't care - that it was there to receive me regardless of my infidelity and my years of estrangement. Its love was unconditional.

Still, I grieved. It had been so long. And I had become so weak without the balancing hand of nature. How could I have been so arrogant to think I could feel whole without coming back to the land and surrendering myself before its grandeur?

And yet, I wondered if I had needed to go without this love for long enough to understand something I once took for granted - if only after those years of separation could I comprehend how sacred this connection was. Hopefully, this time I wouldn't forget so easily.

Eight

As summer was coming to an end, I picked up a second job serving tables part-time at a restaurant in my neighbourhood. This short-term, seasonal gig helped supplement my income during a slow period at my main job.

It was at this new restaurant where I met Sofia. Sofia was a beautiful young woman with long, thick, jet-black hair, a strong Mexican accent, and a fiery intensity to her presence. We seldom worked alongside each other or even spoke on the job, but whenever we crossed paths in the restaurant, I could feel a wild, magnetic energy and tension coming from her that left me confused. If I had to guess what was happening in Sofia based solely on what I was feeling, I would have thought she wanted to grab and kiss me aggressively. But I didn't trust this intuitive hunch - Sofia was much younger than me and lived in a different world. She was a vibrant, superficially stunning young woman who liked to party and enjoy the finer things in life, and I was an introverted, monkish, minimalist writer. It was probably just my imagination or a curious chemistry that meant nothing at the end of the day.

Sofia and I lived in the same neighbourhood, so on nights when we were both working, we sometimes walked home together. During these walks, I learned a little bit about her. In the beginning, our conversations were simple and awkward. I was more stilted and tense than usual due to the raging chemistry burning quietly beneath the surface of our casual interactions. Still, we laughed about life and spoke about what we were looking forward to and feeling challenged by in our worlds. It was fun talking with her.

More significant than any words we exchanged, however, was the energy. There was a chemistry between us that felt dizzying and ungrounding - like a strong wind that threatened to push me off my feet. And it only grew more intense as we shared more walks home.

After one of these walks, I accompanied Sofia to the door of her apartment building, then stumbled back to mine, feeling like there must be some universal force that wanted us to get together - because I didn't understand how that *wasn't* going to happen. The feelings of chemistry and carnal attraction were simply too strong. I always had a rule for myself that I wouldn't get romantically involved with coworkers, and up to this point, it was a rule I had remained faithful to. But I could feel how quickly and easily something might happen with Sofia. It felt volatile in a way that was both exciting and concerning. In a way, it felt inevitable.

Eight

After getting home that night, I fell asleep and dreamed that Sofia and I were having sex. During the dream, Sofia seemed to get hurt somehow and pull away in pain. Then, in the middle of this, I woke up alone in the darkness and silence of my apartment, with a sinking feeling in my gut. As I lay awake, a simple message rang through my head as though it were planted there as a final note from the dream: *Wrong choice.*

My body was filled with the terrible feeling that I'd made a mistake. There was an acrid taste of regret in my mouth and an understanding that however good this physical intimacy had seemed or appeared to be - something about it wasn't right.

"Well, that's not subtle," I thought to myself. For a while, I lay wide awake, accepting that I probably needed to listen to what I was feeling, despite my temptation to do otherwise. I wondered if this was why the chemistry between Sophia and I had made me so dizzy and nervous: It was enjoyable and exciting, but acting on it might be unwise. With this in mind, I accepted that I had better steer myself away from feeding the flame that was developing between us.

After that night, my behaviour around Sofia changed. Instead of trying to walk home together, I tried to avoid it. Instead of making eye contact with her or brushing against her shoulder, I kept my distance when possible. These were subtle shifts in behaviour, but they were my way of changing course.

One evening, near the end of a shift, Sofia asked me what I was doing after work.

"I'm probably going home, having a bite to eat, and then sleeping," I casually responded.

"Let's get something to eat together, then," she said. "Want to?"

I instantly got nervous at this suggestion. I could feel how much I wanted to say yes, but at the same time, I thought that I was supposed to say no. After some reflection and hesitation, I decided hanging out with a new person and being social would be good for me. I reasoned that this would be an opportunity to get to know someone as a friend, nothing more, and decided to challenge my inner loner by saying yes.

After work, we went to a pub in the neighbourhood and chatted about life over food and a drink. We spoke about our love lives. Sofia asked me why I was single and when my last relationship had been. I explained that it had been years since I was involved with anyone romantically - but that some beautiful things had happened during this time. I had been learning about love in all sorts of other ways.

"Wait, you haven't been with anyone in *years?*" she asked, confused. "Like no sex? Nothing?"

"Nothing," I responded. "I haven't kissed someone since before the pandemic."

"That's not healthy," she said in disbelief. "Nothing, for *years!* You need to be touched - it's not good to be so solitary!"

I told her that she was probably right - it probably wasn't a healthy thing. And yet I also shared that these past few years had been one of the most beautiful, happy, and love-filled periods of my life.

"It's fascinating," I explained, "because I think you're correct. And yet I've still had an incredibly rich love life the whole time I've been alone. Even just walking in the woods every morning, I feel like I'm in a love relationship with something - like I'm exchanging love in a very real and satisfying way. And I feel that with friends, too. And at work - in all kinds of social situations. It's like, I think that not being able to experience love in that one potent way, with a lover, has forced me to learn how to give and receive it in all these other places. And I'm not lying - I'm not pretending - I'm dead serious. It's been beautiful."

"Okay, if you say so," Sofia remarked skeptically, and we laughed.

After eating, we walked to the water, sat on the beach together, and continued speaking. I learned more about Sofia's life in Mexico and what moving to Canada alone as a young woman was like. I admired the bravery and conviction that such an adventurous choice would have taken.

As our conversation meandered, Sofia made a passing comment that caught my attention: "I've noticed how easy it is for you to get angry. It's too easy. The little things get you."

The bluntness and transparency of this statement caught me off guard, and something about it seemed significant - so I asked her to explain what she meant in greater detail.

Sofia described a couple of situations at work where I had become flustered and frustrated temporarily. Little things with a coworker or a customer I was serving that triggered me, which she'd noticed. It was uncomfortable and surprising to be called out in such a direct way for these moments of poor composure and reactivity - but I also found it fascinating and wanted to hear her thoughts and observations. After all, this was someone who had been watching me in the unfiltered motions of my daily life.

"It just doesn't make sense," she explained. "Because you're the nicest person - you are always kind and sweet. And then, for no good reason, you become angry. It's strange because when you're angry, it doesn't feel like you - it doesn't match you. And then, a few seconds later, it's over, and you're back. The anger doesn't last long, but it's intense. It's strange."

Sofia may have just been making conversation without realizing how deeply her words would touch a self-conscious part of me. I had spent so many years raking myself over the coals for getting emotionally triggered and being reactive that it was hard to take her passing observations lightly. Part of me was ready to leap into a pit of self-loathing and shame, but I did my best to stay where I was sitting - to listen and remain curious.

I acknowledged to Sophia that I knew what she was talking about and had been working on it, but I still had my regular moments of weakness.

"It's not that bad," Sofia replied, perhaps sensing the grave tone I had taken around this subject. "It's just surprising," she continued. "I expect everyone else to act like that, but I wouldn't expect it from you."

"Well, I'm weak and childish, too," I said, and we laughed.

As we continued talking, I thought to myself how interesting it was that Sofia, of all people, had made this observation about me. She was a fiery, assertive personality herself - someone who could conjure formidable anger very easily. As our conversation continued, she even asked for my advice on a recent conflict with a coworker who got upset with her and said she was too aggressive and arrogant.

"I guess we're not that different," I thought out loud. "The thing about your fiery personality, Sofia, is that it might be really helpful to you in life. That inner fire, that ability to get angry, it's probably what gave you the courage to move across the world by yourself to a country where you didn't know a single person. That's a scary thing, and I bet that your fiery personality helps you blaze a path. It'll probably help you accomplish lots of dreams in life and push you toward the scary things you want. I mean, you asked me to hang out tonight because you're assertive and fiery."

"That's true. I am a strong woman," she said, laughing.

"Something like that might be true for me, too," I continued. "I have this fire in me, and I have to be careful with it, or it can hurt people and make a mess - but I think it might be a beautiful thing if I use it wisely."

"It's not a bad thing," Sofia agreed.

It was late now, and Sofia - wearing just a tiny mini-skirt and flip-flops, was freezing in the cold, damp ocean air. There had been several points where it could have made sense to cuddle up and keep her warm with my body or invite her back to my place. It seemed as though the night had been perfectly orchestrated for this - and it was almost painful to not go in that direction. But something in me said *don't*. So I offered to walk her home.

When we got to her apartment building, Sofia gave me a long, tender hug that almost melted me. Her lips pressed into the nape of my neck, sending waves of euphoria tingling down my spine, and before that could become something more, I took a deep breath, stepped back, and thanked her for a beautiful evening.

The following morning, I went for an early walk in the forest as Sofia's words from the beach echoed through my thoughts: *You get angry too easily.*

The way she had delivered that observation was so blunt and direct it had been emblazoned in my mind, and I couldn't help but meditate and reflect on what she'd seen in me and called attention to. There was a certain quality to those words that made it feel as though something was speaking through her in that moment of our conversation - as though life itself had used Sofia as a messenger for a particularly vital message.

As I slowly walked along the forest path, I reflected on moments of moodiness at work, instances of frustration and irritability, and examples of reacting to little things that I knew didn't matter. I acknowledged how easy it was for me to get angry, and I wondered why.

Then, a thought flashed into my awareness - almost like a direct answer that surprised me: *You're getting angry because you aren't doing what you should be doing with your life. You won't be happy unless you're creating, taking risks, and challenging yourself - you can't be.*

For a few months at this point, I had taken a break from writing, making podcasts, etc, and I had noticed on many occasions a direct correlation between my creative stagnation and my irritability, reactivity, and neurotic patterns. Writing and creative work were ways of taking my inner fire and directing it into something healthy and productive. Without doing that consistently, the fire started burning in troublesome ways. I would become angsty, judgemental, entitled, and volatile. A deep part of me would feel like he was carrying a chip on his shoulder - like he was being held back in life - because he was. But he would get angry at the world when it was just me holding myself back due to fear and insecurity.

Walking along that forest trail, I found it comforting to think that I might never be happy unless I was engaged in meaningful, creative work - that my anger might be a guardian angel making sure I knew whenever I broke a promise with myself - whenever I strayed too far away from my truth.

For years, I tried to outsmart my anger. I thought it was a negative emotion to overcome. And yet every attempt to overcome it had been futile - it was a force of nature. To look at it with more respect - as an inner fire, a messenger letting me know there was something I needed to do, tend to, or change, felt more realistic.

I wondered if my restlessness and inability to be a happy, well-adjusted person *without* pushing past my procrastination and creative blocks was one of the greatest gifts I could be blessed with. There was no peace without turning toward the vulnerability of living fully.

In the weeks after that conversation with Sofia, I began writing regularly again. As I did this, I noticed an immediate shift in my emotional reactivity. I still had a fragile ego - it was just a bit calmer. Because I was battling procrastination and sparring with creative ideas, I was less inclined to pick fights with the many imperfections of daily life. My inner fire had a place to go and direct its energy - a place to burn. I still had my moments, but something felt much calmer. A deep part of me didn't feel oppressed and held back by life - because I wasn't holding myself back.

By the time fall arrived, my main job had gotten busy again, and I left Sofia's workplace. We never went for a second dinner together, and our chemistry never resulted in more than that conversation on the beach.

Although we only crossed paths for a brief moment, I felt that Sofia had given me something important. Her fiery, assertive personality pointed out how my fiery personality could get twisted. Her presence made me look inward and got me onto a streak of creative activity.

And something else interesting happened during our conversation on the beach that night: When Sofia told me that I get angry too easily, I felt intensely ashamed and defensive. A self-preservation impulse got triggered in me as I was confronted by the blunt impact of her words. I felt like I was being called out and put on blast - like I was being judged and seen as a bad person who wasn't liked.

While I was having this reaction, I noticed something peculiar: Although Sofia was pointing out a weakness of mine, she had also chosen to be with me that night. She had invited me to dinner. She wanted to spend time with me. She liked me.

Holding these two realities together: That a weakness of mine was being seen and named, and yet I was still being liked - felt very significant. To be imperfect and still be accepted was an extraordinary feeling. It was hard to let in, and it kind of felt like the best thing ever.

Nine

I was alone in my apartment one September night when I decided to turn off the lights, close my eyes, and meditate. It had been a busy few months, and I hadn't been in the habit of sitting in silence for a while - it seemed like a good time to be quiet and still.

As I settled and relaxed, countless thoughts flowed through my mind. I was trying to stay present, focus on my breath, and avoid being carried away by my inner dialogue (a stream of worry, gossip, catchy songs, etc.), but one passing thought caught my attention: It was my Grandma. I had not thought about Grandma in years, but for some reason, she came to mind - I felt a memory of her presence so vivid it caught me off guard.

Curious why Grandma had popped into this meditation, I let my focus wander in her direction, shifting my centre of attention from my breath to her.

Then, almost immediately, something happened: I felt the love of my Grandmother pour into me like an enormous river. I couldn't see my Grandma's face. I couldn't hear her voice speaking words - but I could feel her love, and it felt monumental. Tears began to stream down my cheeks. It felt like Grandma's love was right there with me, around me, and holding me.

As this feeling poured through my body, I saw visions of silver-white energy in my mind's eye - the colour Grandma's hair had been during my childhood. I noticed how the nurturing energy I felt in that moment matched her affectionate presence many years earlier - the unflinching love she had beamed with pride at her grandchildren. The longer I let myself sit and feel this energy, the more I recognized its familiarity: *This is what Grandma felt like. This was what her energy did when she sat beside you on the couch watching TV. It glowed like this - it felt unconditional like this.*

I had forgotten. By now, I was crying heavily as this energy held me, moved through me, and reminded me of something.

It had been years since I thought about Grandma and decades since she passed away (when I was nine years old). As an adult, I had mainly remembered her as a fiery woman - someone who was maybe a bit harsh. I often focused on how different we were - how I chose a creative, adventurous, spiritual path in contrast to her more conservative, conventional life. For some reason, I typically only remembered Grandma's negative qualities and never gave much thought to her positive ones. I never thought much about the unlimited love she had showered on my brothers and me as children. It was as though I had closed off from that reality after she died. Maybe that was a way of dealing with my confusing feelings. And maybe, as I grew older, I learned to expect love and wisdom to come in certain forms, which she didn't embody - so I failed to recognize the immaculate example of them she had held in plain sight.

Now, for the first time since she died, I felt the immensity of her love. At that moment, something opened up, and I could see it - I could let it in. It felt like the purest love imaginable. It felt like someone had been watching me - like *she* had been watching me - for my entire life. I got the sense she had witnessed everything I had done since she passed away: Every lie I told. Every cruel word I spoke. Everything I stole. Every time I did something selfless or kind for no reason. Every horrible, brave, and decent thing. She'd been watching, witnessing it all, and loved me just the same. Her heart was steady and unflinching. To feel so seen and exposed, yet still loved without a flicker of hesitation or judgment, blew my mind.

I sat there and cried for a long time, letting the enormity of these feelings in. I couldn't believe how I had forgotten this love - how I had closed myself off from it and lost sight of what a gorgeous, angelic example of acceptance my Grandmother was.

I wondered if she really had been watching me all these years (at that moment, it certainly felt like it). I remembered dozens of synchronicities and little miracles, moments of magical good fortune or strange protection throughout my life. I wondered if Grandma had been involved in them - if she'd been looking out for me. At that moment, it felt like she had been. It felt like she had always been here - like she never left. It felt like I had her presence and support throughout my life, the same way I had it when I was a child. It felt like her love had never gone anywhere - it had never died.

For the next month, I could feel my Grandmother's presence whenever I meditated. I felt her energy and saw that silver-white imagery in my mind's eye. The feeling of her unconditional, nurturing love was like an antidote to the pain of daily life - a healing balm to soothe and displace my shame, self-doubt, and inner criticism. It was a reminder of a powerful love I had forgotten - stable, wise, and supportive. It was pleased with me simply living, being happy, and being Miles. Nothing fancy or sophisticated mattered, and nothing needed to be achieved or proven to earn or sustain this love. To just be, was enough.

I could also feel my Grandmother's presence in my daily life. It was like she was around and close by - like I had reopened a relationship, and we were getting to know each other again. I felt supported, lifted, and strengthened by the spirit of her love.

Over time, the intensity of her presence began to fade. I didn't feel it the same when I sat down to meditate - it diminished. And then, one day, it was gone. She no longer felt close by - I couldn't feel her presence or support lifting me.

Nine

I accepted that this was probably part of a process. Perhaps I had received something I badly needed from her, and it had been delivered in full.

One morning during this time, I received a Facebook friend request from an old acquaintance I hadn't spoken to in many years named Heather. I was surprised and happy to see Heather's smiling face in her profile photo and immediately accepted her request.

As I scrolled through her posts, it quickly became clear that Heather was not doing well. It appeared that she was in an advanced stage of cancer. Her latest posts were all heartbreaking updates about chemotherapy, surgery, infections, and the breakdown of bodily functions. As I scrolled along, saw her photos, and read her tortured words, I realized that Heather was dying. In one of her posts, she recounted the advice of an oncologist who encouraged her to transition out of treatment and into a hospice for end-of-life care.

Ever the rebellious spirit, Heather was not ready to give up so easily. She had spent years learning about herbal medicine and alternative healing and was driven to explore therapeutic paths her oncologist was unaware of. She had a warrior spirit.

But in the words of her posts, there was a trembling vulnerability. She knew things were serious, and she was afraid of dying.

When I first met Heather, I was twenty years old, and she was about the same age. We were both wide-eyed youths, in love with the magic of nature, figuring out how to thrust ourselves into that realm as deeply as possible. We crossed paths at a gathering of mutual friends - she was a traveller who, at the time, had no home. A hippy - a faerie-like punk with hand-sewn, earth-toned clothing, a tiny physical frame, and a mane of long, thick, fire-red hair that matched her vibrant personality.

I had a crush on Heather almost immediately after meeting her. She was creative, wild, mysterious, and intimidating in her intelligence - I was in awe of her.

It always felt like there was a magnetism between us, a silent, unspoken feeling of mutual affection that we were both probably too shy to ever act on.

For a period of several years, I would run into Heather occasionally. Never for long, and usually by surprise, but we ended up befriending some of the same people and visiting some of the same places. Whenever these chance meetings occurred, it felt like we knew each other in some unspoken way - that silent feeling of admiration was always there.

The last time I had seen her was over a decade earlier. I was living on a piece of forested land with a group of friends at the time, one of whom was close to Heather and invited her to stay with us for a few days. It was spring, and Heather spent most of her time during that visit outside - drawing, painting, and weaving cedar bark baskets with our mutual friend, Ella. I cannot remember a single conversation we had during that visit, but I still remember the feeling we shared - that silent feeling of admiration. It felt like we both saw the beauty in each other and that if life was different, we could have been partners - we could have fallen in love.

But life was not different, and Heather disappeared again after that. I would hear stories about her adventures over the years (for a while, rumour had it that she was a nomadic goat herder in northern California), but I lost all contact with her.

Now, scrolling through her Facebook profile and reading scary words like chemotherapy, mastectomy, metastasize, and terminal, I was shaken. I had known Heather as an unstoppable beam of light - a magical young traveller who was fiercely independent, would take shit from no one, and was a ball of unpredictable creative energy. Seeing what cancer had done to her - how it had drained the life from her body - was hard for me to wrap my head around.

As the gravity of Heather's situation sunk in, I wondered: Why did she reach out to me now? It looked like Heather might be very close to the end. Was there something important she had to say to me? Was there something I needed to tell her?

After sitting with this question for a while, I decided I would write her. It made no sense to hold anything back, so I sat down and composed a simple message. I told her how much of an impression she made on me all those years ago, how special she was, and how although our lives barely touched (I honestly couldn't remember a single conversation we ever had), I always felt admiration for her.

It was a simple, heartfelt message of praise and support. When I finished it, I decided to hold onto it briefly before hitting send. Heather's updates made it clear that she was in so much physical pain everything felt like torture. I wondered if, given the stress and discomfort she was in, my message would be an unnecessary burden. With that thought in mind, I held onto it.

Days passed, and the urgency with which I had written those words to Heather faded. I felt more and more that it would probably be best to not bother Heather at all - to send my love and appreciation to her through prayer or warm thoughts. I deleted the message before hitting send.

Heather's social media posts continued every few days. Sometimes, they were hopeful. Sometimes, they were frustrated, terrified, and confused. Then, one afternoon as I walked through the front door to start a shift at work, I got an email. It was an update from a GoFundMe campaign for Heather's medical expenses that I'd donated to. Heather had passed away.

I felt shocked, sad, and relieved that she was out of her pain. As I walked up a flight of stairs and into a busy restaurant, that news knocked the wind out of me.

Nine

In the days that followed, I thought about Heather a lot. I wondered again: Why did she appear in my world at the end of her life? Why did she connect with me? Should I have written her? My first instinct had been to reach out, to say hello and send some love her way. But now that ship had sailed, and I missed my chance - I let my self-consciousness get in the way again. I rationalized to myself that I held back from writing her because of empathy and consideration for her weakened state. But still, I had a feeling it was probably the wrong choice.

On one of my morning walks in the woods, I reflected on things I could have said to Heather if I had gotten over myself. Then, I realized I could say it all to her at that moment - I could tell her how special she was. Everything I had wanted to say then, I could say now.

So as I walked along the forest path, I had a silent conversation with Heather. I shared what an impression she made on me - how I admired her unique, intelligent, vibrant example of living. I shared how her strong and rebellious spirit had inspired me, how her defiant weirdness had made me feel less alone, and how the sense of acceptance and respect I received from her made me feel seen - it meant a lot. There was sincerity and warmth to everything I expressed - sharing all the positive feelings and memories I had of her as though she was there.

Then, I noticed something that surprised me. It was like Heather *was* there. In a similar way to how my Grandma had been with me when I meditated on her, it was like I had been having a conversation with Heather, and now I could feel her right there, beside me on that trail.

Heather's presence felt so strong that it was like she was communicating with me non-verbally - like her energy was speaking to me.

I felt her love and admiration. It was as though she was answering my words of praise for her, with her own praise back in my direction: I felt how Heather believed in me and my life more than maybe anyone. She believed in my writing - she believed it would change the world. She believed my work was sacred and beautiful - a man tearing himself open. She believed in me so much it was almost confusing - it was so beautiful and foreign.

As I continued walking, I felt Heather's fiery personality with me, cheering me on and showering me with a warrior-like spirit of enthusiasm, support, and eagerness. She wanted me to flourish, to spread my gifts as far and wide as possible. She felt like a soldier, a strong woman, rooting for me and goading me along my life path.

It also felt like Heather wanted me to date women. There was a sense that she was laughing at me and shaking her head in disbelief at my celibacy and total lack of romantic activity. This aspect of my life made no sense to her. Again, it seemed like she really believed in me - she thought I was a good man and that it was insane for me to not share myself with someone. She wanted me to be out there, getting some action and sharing my love. It made me laugh.

Nine

This feeling of Heather's presence did not fade quickly. It felt like I was having an inner conversation with her for the rest of that morning's walk - like I had the support of a beloved friend by my side. And this friend saw me in ways I had forgotten were possible.

Days passed, and when I went for my morning walks in the woods, I continued to feel Heather - her presence did not fade. I started to feel a giddy excitement and anticipation about our connection - the way I remembered feeling toward a new lover. There was an openness, curiosity, and chemistry that felt ecstatic. To feel seen in such a generous way by a fiercely independent, strong, and intelligent spirit was a healing salve for my battered sense of self.

As this connection continued, I realized that Heather was the first woman I had felt a strong romantic connection with during this life who had died. While nothing ever even came close to happening between us romantically, Heather and I had a chemistry - a resonance - that was rare. It felt like we just knew each other on some soul level (despite the reality that, as people, we knew almost nothing about one another).

I wondered if this post-mortem connection I felt with her was because we had forged a particular kind of emotional or spiritual bond while she was alive. In a small way, we exchanged a very direct feeling of love (and perhaps there is no small way of doing that).

Now that she had passed on, maybe that connection still existed. Maybe that love didn't die - it sure didn't feel like it.

One day during a walk, as I felt Heather's presence with me, I realized how easy it would be to fall in love with her and avoid the challenge of being with a living woman. It felt like a distinct path I could walk down - sinking into this gorgeous connection with someone no one else could see or understand. The moment I saw this possibility, I got the impression it was a wrong choice - something gratuitous and off-balance. It felt like Heather might have had the same insight - although her presence did not immediately vanish.

Over the following weeks, due to the distractions of life or something else I don't fully understand, the feeling of Heather's presence faded away. If I sat down and meditated, I could still push myself to feel her radiance, warmth, and support. But for the most part, it was gone. During my morning walks, I was alone again. Life returned to normal.

And strangely, I didn't resist this. Although the feelings of love and encouragement I received during that window of connection to Heather were extraordinary, it felt like I had received a gift in full - like something had been exchanged.

Ten

In mid-fall, I travelled to a small coastal town for a book-related speaking event at a local library. This was the first talk I had been able to arrange at a public library since my book's publication, and I was excited to be doing something conventional as an author to promote my work.

As the event approached, I did some simple promotion and wondered what kind of turnout to expect - though the most important thing seemed to be that I push myself and do things like this, not that they be well attended or superficially successful.

On the day of the event, I spent several hours travelling by bus and ferry, carrying a heavy box of books to sell to attendees at the talk that evening. I brought a notebook into which I scribbled thoughts and mapped out what I would speak about at the library as I sat in transit.

When I arrived at my destination, there were still a couple of hours before the presentation was scheduled to begin, so I decided to grab something to eat and enjoy the sunny autumn afternoon outside.

When I finally made my way to the library, I met and shook hands with the librarian, Matt, who had helped me organize the event. He was an incredibly kind young man about my age, and we exchanged some warm words as he showed me to the area that he had prepared for my talk. With no early arrivals, we both wondered what kind of crowd there would be. By this point, I had emotionally braced myself for anything, including the possibility of nobody showing up.

As we spoke, Matt shared that he was a writer himself, and we ended up chatting about his creative process and work while I set up a little display of books for attendees to look at. We slipped into a natural, easy conversation, and before I knew it, the event's start time had come and gone, and nobody had shown up.

By this point, I was in such a good mood that I didn't feel embarrassed or disappointed. It was almost like I couldn't afford to feel ashamed by this turn of events. My shame would have been too happy to feast on the vulnerability of this situation and tear me to pieces. So another part of me - my sense of humour and fun - almost automatically pushed my cynical, negative inner voices to the side. I laughed about the reality of being a fledgling, self-published author and spoke to Matt honestly about how unsuccessful and bumpy my path with this new book had been.

Then, fifteen minutes after the event was slated to begin, an excited young woman walked across the library toward us. She had a smile across her face as she approached and seemed unfazed by the empty seats in front of Matt and me.

For a moment, I felt a pang of horror and embarrassment, realizing that one person showing up to this event was much more shameful than nobody showing up at all - for that one person was now a witness to the failure on display. Before she had arrived, this was a secret that only Matt and I knew about. Now, she knew.

Before that thought could take hold of me, this young woman introduced herself and stretched out her hand to shake mine. Her name was Marissa, and she explained that she'd recently read my book and was very moved by it. She had driven nearly an hour to attend the talk and was excited to ask some questions that the book had stirred up in her.

After a few minutes of chatting, I realized that I wouldn't be giving a presentation that night - it made more sense to sit down with Marissa and just chat. So, for the next hour, we spoke about the book and what it had meant to her. We talked about where she was at in her life and where I was in mine. I was touched by her kind words regarding the book and extremely curious to speak with a stranger about their impressions of something so close to me.

As we chatted, I acknowledged the awkwardness and humour of that moment: She was the only person to show up to my event - the sole witness to this moment of public embarrassment. And yet somehow, it felt perfect. The one person who showed up had something so positive and touching to share. And because it was just the two of us, we got to sit down and have a sincere, one-on-one conversation for an hour. I got to hear about the realities of her life and get a feel for who she was. And she got the same - it was a special opportunity.

While we talked, I felt a fire being lit inside me. By the end of our conversation, I began to feel like this event was an extraordinary success. Not in a superficial way - on an entirely different level. I had gotten to connect with this beautiful person. But more than anything, I had the extraordinary experience of forcing myself to do something scary and having it fail. One person showed up. I carried my heavy box of books there and would carry it home, still full. And yet I didn't think about giving up or feeling discouraged for a second. Disappointment didn't enter into the conversation. I felt emboldened and excited that I could try something, have an underwhelming response, and want more. I was getting a taste of what my ego called failure, and it was actually really good. It made me hungry.

After a long conversation, Marissa and I exchanged a hug and said goodbye before she left the empty library. With her gone, Matt returned from his desk, and together we stacked up the rows of unused chairs he had kindly arranged for me before the event. As we spoke, Matt empathized with my struggle as a fledgling author and wished more people had turned up for me. He was very gracious and encouraging, and as our conversation continued, we spoke about his job at the library and his writing some more. When it came time for me to run and catch my bus home, I thanked Matt for everything, gave him a copy of my book, shook his hand, and said goodbye.

As I stepped out of that library, I felt like I was about to explode with excitement. My eyes were wider than usual, and I was filled with energy. It was like the experience of walking through this public failure had awakened something in me, and I suddenly felt incredibly alive. Maybe it was that I faced a fear *(What if nobody comes to this? What if nobody cares about this?)*, and on the other side of that was a phenomenal sense of freedom *(What if I don't care?)*.

Sure, the seats were nearly all empty, and I never did give that talk I planned out. But I made two new friends and had deep, soulful interactions with them. It was beautiful.

In the wake of that event, I wanted to feel more of what I'd just touched (risk, failure, and devotion to a vision regardless of immediate results). A sense of confidence and aspiration had come alive in me - a welcome reprieve from some of the insecurities of my everyday inner life. I wasn't entirely sure what to do with all this energy and confidence, but it felt amazing.

At the end of the fall, I went back home to visit my parents for the weekend. I had been invited to do a reading at a book fair in the area and decided to attend the event as an excuse to make the trip and see my family.

The first day of my visit was consumed by the book fair, which mainly consisted of sitting behind a table displaying my books on it and starting conversations with strangers. There was something wonderfully awkward and exposing about sitting there, initiating interactions with passersby, and learning how to talk about myself and my work without shame or embarrassment.

On the second evening, my parents invited my older brother and his wife over for dinner, and we sat around the kitchen table for a few hours talking about family, the state of the world, and old times. After everyone left and my Mom went to bed, I joined my Dad as he watched TV in the living room. There was something incredibly nostalgic about this scene - as a child, the endless hours of sitting with him in that room in front of the TV seemed meaningless and forgettable. But now, there was something precious about every moment sitting there with him.

He was watching a documentary about Willie Nelson and explained to me what a good guy Willie was. My Dad had a couple of drinks in him by this point, and his usual conversational self was even more open and gregarious than normal. So as the TV played random shows in the background, we talked.

We spoke about my cousins, dead uncles, long-gone grandparents, and great-grandparents. I had questions about all of these people I was connected to so deeply - these people who probably struggled with some of the same demons and had some of the same hopes as me.

Ten

The conversation swung far and wide, jumping from one topic to another. At one point, my Dad made a passing comment about my book. He mentioned that he disagreed with how I depicted my childhood in it, with a quiet pain in his voice, before quickly moving on to another subject.

But the pain in his voice was too much for me to ignore. I knew I wanted to talk to him about it, but as he moved on with the conversation, I wondered how.

Over a year earlier, I sent my parents a copy of my new book, hoping they might enjoy it. I knew a couple of things in it might be difficult for them to read - passing comments about childhood experiences and their lasting imprints on me. But the book was not about my childhood or my parents. There was only one moment when I spoke directly about my upbringing - but it happened to be on the book's very first page and was pretty unflattering. On that first page, I described a passing scene from my adolescence where I was afraid of my Dad and resented him. I painted this picture with the gravitas and emotional intensity of my thirteen-year-old self's angst. I described how life felt as a kid who didn't understand the complexity of what his father might go through and feel sometimes.

When my Dad got that book in the mail, he sat on the couch by himself, opened it up, and read those painful words on the first page. He read a story about his son fearing him, a story that depicted him as an angry man.

He was shaken when I spoke to him a few days after he finished reading the book. Those opening words, while they occupied a tiny, passing moment of the long story contained in its pages, hurt him. He felt misunderstood, exposed, and read the rest of the book from that place. When he reached the end of it (and a kind of resolution to everything), he acknowledged that he was touched and felt much better. But as we spoke, it was clear that my words had been a gut punch.

I realized I should have talked about the book with him before sending that copy. I should have told him it shared some emotionally charged memories from my childhood - but that it was a story which only looked at such things on its way to a place of love and understanding. At the time, I had been too nervous and distracted to think through how my words might affect him and gave him no warning or preface.

When we spoke immediately after he read it, I explained that I didn't resent him at all in the present moment and that my intention with the book was not to paint him or anyone in a negative light. I thought that the teenage angst and resentment I described were nearly universal feelings that kids have towards their parents and that while it would have been difficult for him to hear, it wasn't unusual and didn't reflect poorly on him as a man or father.

It was a difficult conversation, and I tried my best to explain to my Dad that I loved him, respected him, and appreciated him. But I understood how those few words must have been painful for him to read.

After several conversations over the following months, we got to a place where my Dad said he understood, that it was all good, and I didn't need to worry about it. There was nothing more to talk about, he said. And yet his words didn't feel like they were fully at peace. It felt unfinished.

Now, sitting with my Dad talking late into the night with the TV playing in the background, I recognized the pain in his voice again. When he mentioned my book in passing, I heard something behind his words that I couldn't ignore. And as he moved on and continued talking about another subject, I fell into a moment of reflection. A voice in me said: *Stop the conversation now. Talk about what you just felt. Ask him if he's still hurt.*

It felt embarrassing and awkward to interrupt the flow of the conversation and forcefully steer it back towards a subject that both of us would be more comfortable skirting past. But the voice wouldn't go away:

DO IT! YOU HAVE TO CONFRONT THIS - YOU'LL REGRET IT FOREVER IF YOU DON'T.

It was a voice I knew I couldn't ignore. So I took a breath, felt a sickening nervousness in my gut, and interrupted my father.

"Hey, Dad, I just noticed that when you mentioned my book, it felt like you still have hurt feelings, and like something I have to acknowledge and talk about."

"Oh," my Dad responded, surprised by my directness. "No, no, we've talked about that already, Miles. It's all good."

I could still hear the pain in his voice, though - it wasn't subtle.

"Okay," I responded. "But I don't believe you. I need you to know that what I wrote in that book was just a little story - the opening page that painted you in such a bad light was me speaking from the voice of my thirteen-year-old self. That's not even remotely close to how I feel about you today. I love you, Dad. I respect you so much. I'm proud of you. I brag to my friends about you. Really."

"It's fine, Miles," he interrupted, "we're all good. We've talked about it before - I don't need anything more with it."

I still heard the pain in his voice. It felt like nothing I said was getting in - like he couldn't let it in - I had hurt his feelings with that book, and there was a wall up. So I continued.

"Okay, I hear you, and I appreciate it. But I still don't feel like what I need to get through to you has gotten through. So I will keep saying this for as long as I need to until I feel like you get it: I love you. I don't wish you were anyone other than who you are. I don't wish you had done anything differently as a father. I mean this. I am grateful to have had you as a Dad. For a while, I got caught up focusing on everything that wasn't good and hurt me about my childhood, which was healthy up to a point - though I think I probably got carried away with it. But now, on the other side of that, I'm being honest when I say it's like I cleaned that stuff out. I don't resent you anymore at all. It's just love here."

I looked directly at him as I continued: "That's all I have now. And I will keep saying this and bringing this conversation up for as long as it takes."

"Okay, if you're being real, I'll be real too," my Dad responded. His voice had changed now - it felt like what I said was getting through.

"I think you got caught up in something bad," he continued. "I think you and Kevin had a way of looking at the negative in people. He would see something in them that wasn't perfect, and that's all he would focus on - it's all he would see. He wouldn't see the whole person, just their flaws. And that's what you got caught up in - you started seeing just the flaws. You started just seeing yourself as a bad person, too - just flaws. I don't think that's who you are, though. *I know you.* That was something you took on, that you got convinced was true - that you're this bad guy who needs to fix himself. But that's not you."

Surprised by the clarity of my Dad's analysis, I thought for a moment before responding: "I think you're right. I agree. It was like a bad trip, focusing so much on the negative in myself and others. It was horrible."

Now, we were both being honest. My Dad continued sharing his feelings: "I knew you as a kid, Miles. You were happy. We had so much fun together! I just remember all of the good times. We went fishing and camping - there was so much fun and love. But all of a sudden, you could only remember the pain. And the way you started talking about yourself as a bad person made no sense to me."

"I know. It was like I stirred up all the pain, and it was the only thing I could see for a while," I admitted.

"You learned a lot through all of that and from Kevin," he continued. "There were a lot of good things that happened. But I just think it got too negative."

"I can't argue with that," I agreed.

The conversation continued for another hour or more. With our guards down, we talked more honestly than I could remember. We both cried, laughed, and cursed. Nothing was off limits. I learned more about my father that night than ever before.

Eventually, I hugged him and made my way to bed. As I lay wide awake, buzzing from the conversation that had just transpired, I wondered about my choices. I wondered about my years of isolation from my family. I wondered about my writing and how aspects of it might have been carelessly honest or transparent. And I also got the sense that the extraordinary conversation I just had with my father would not have happened without all of these things.

Without my friend Kevin and our years of exploration together, I would not have noticed the voice in my head pushing me to be honest with my father about what I was feeling. I might not have even noticed what I was feeling in the first place. Without those years of isolation, I would not have understood or outgrown my inner voices of resentment towards my Dad. As much as I could look back at my choices with regret, I also had to acknowledge how the beauty of this moment was born from them.

The following morning, when I got up and wandered into the kitchen, my Mom was sitting there reading a mystery novel. Without looking up from the page she was on, she heard my footsteps and commented: "Good morning. Sounds like you and your father had a great conversation last night."

We did.

On the last evening of my stay, I watched a nature documentary with my parents and went to bed at a more reasonable hour than the previous night. While I slept in my childhood bedroom, I had an interesting dream. In it, my mother gave me some relationship advice. This was quite out of character for her, as neither of my parents ever inquired about my love life, let alone offered guidance on finding a mate. I think they just assumed I was marching to the beat of my own drum, and they had two other sons that were married, so there was no pressure on me to settle down or find a partner.

In the dream, my mother said: "*Miles, you need to just start being with women. Just start sleeping with people. Go on dates. Stop trying to wait for the perfect thing to come along. Stop trying to become perfect before you give yourself experiences. You have to just start getting out there - that's how you'll find your person eventually. You have to get the ball rolling, step out into the world, meet people, have sex, and you'll be surprised at what you find. You'll be surprised at who you end up having feelings for. That's how it works.*"

It was the first time I had gotten relationship advice from my Mom as an adult, and it was certainly not what I would have expected: Have sex. Just give yourself experiences, and don't try to control them.

Something about that perspective felt very wise - wiser than me.

Several weeks after returning home from that visit with my parents, I decided it was time for another mushroom trip. I had continued spacing my experiments with mushrooms apart by at least one month, trying to approach them (and my mental stability) with the utmost respect. One of these experiences left me with a residual feeling of mental fragility and disorientation that was scary and a bit disturbing. It lasted for a week or so and caused me to pause and reconsider if, how, or when I would continue exploring with mushrooms.

Enough time had passed since that episode that I felt mentally stable and resilient again, and a moderate dose of mushrooms seemed responsible and felt right. The only thing I thought I might be doing wrong was continuing to take mushrooms alone. It sounded like the general advice was to only take moderate to higher doses of mushrooms in the presence of trustworthy peers. I knew it probably wasn't ideal to be doing this solo, but it was a risk and a compromise that I was comfortable subjecting myself to.

During a day off from work with no other plans or commitments, I felt that the time was right. I skipped breakfast and ate some dried mushrooms on an empty stomach (having been told by a friend that this would lead to a more potent high).

A few minutes after washing down the crunchy dried mushrooms with some water, I decided to head out into the crisp winter morning and get into the woods to set the tone for this experience. As I made my way into the park and got further from my home, I wondered if I might get too high to be outside in the frosty cold forest alone, but I figured I would cross that bridge when I got there.

Walking along my usual morning route, I noticed something that surprised me: It had only been about twenty minutes since I ate those mushrooms, but reality was bending and twisting in a very peculiar way already. My mind was suddenly hit by a wave, and everything in its wake was clearer, more alive, beautiful, and distorted. I was really damn high.

This was happening much faster and with greater intensity than I was expecting. So much so that it felt like my consciousness could launch out of my body and into the emptiness of space at any moment. Realizing how exposed I was in the freezing cold on a public trail, I decided I had better get home before this got even more intense.

For the next fifteen minutes, I strained to maintain some semblance of ordinary consciousness as I power-walked home. Sunlight filtered into the forest and made every frost-covered tree, leaf, and twig glow with a stunning aliveness that almost demanded I stop and stare. The cedar trees looked seductive, nearly convincing me to stay out in the beauty of this living world. But the frozen puddles reminded me that it was no longer summer, and the strength of what I was feeling suggested that this might be a more disorienting high than anything I had experienced with mushrooms yet.

As I got to the park's edge, I walked past a stand of dead hydrangea flowerheads and saw them as completely enlightened beings. I could see and feel them emanating energy like breath in the empty space around their bushy bodies. I wondered what the hell I was doing, rushing back to my apartment's lifeless, pathetic reality. Still, I carried on.

When I finally got to my apartment, I was grateful that I had kept my mind grounded and together long enough to make it there, and I told myself that it was okay to fall to pieces now.

After taking off my shoes and winter coat, I sat on my futon and was instantly hit with absolute horror at the scene before me. I stared across the tiny room at my messy desktop. There was a sweater and a t-shirt thrown carelessly on top of it, along with piles of disorganized books, notes, cables, etc. It was in disarray. Normally, this wouldn't bother me. But in the wildly heightened state of sensitivity that had just enabled me to see the perfect enlightened truth of decaying flowerheads, I was repulsed by the horrific ugliness of my messy apartment.

The disorganized recycling placed carelessly on my kitchen counter. The unswept floor. Every minor, careless detail that wouldn't usually be offensive felt like a sacrilegious betrayal of the divine.

This scene put me in a state of shock and disbelief at the failure of my life. I saw my disorganized apartment as a reflection of a man who was off track - a man who didn't care about the little things - as if they weren't all part of something urgently important and sacred.

A voice began speaking to me - and it didn't stop for the next several hours: *"You're squandering your life,"* it said. *"Just look. Everything is sacred, and you've lost the way. Look!"*

In that moment of horror, I was painfully aware that the beautiful vibrant harmony so apparent in the forest was missing from my living environment. There was a simple natural grace and order that I had neglected to implement here. My apartment wasn't a disaster, but it wasn't being cared for in a sacred way. It was a manifestation of my neglect - a sobering reflection of my unlived potential. I was a writer who wasn't writing every day. I was capable of living and loving more fully, and yet I could spend days squandering my time in idleness and apathy. I felt the heaviness of this reality and, for a moment, wondered if I should have stayed out in the faery playground of the forest. It would have been much more blissful.

But as I sat and burned, I knew I needed to feel this. There was more in me to give to this life, and caring for my living environment as though it was a sacred garden was something I had simply forgotten to do.

"You deserve more," the voice said. *"You must give yourself more beauty in life - surround yourself with it. What you see in the forest, bring it everywhere!"*

After sitting with this crushing reality for a while, my attention shifted. I sat in silence, eyes closed, as scenes of fetal development, childhood insecurity, and the complex emotions of being a middle sibling flashed through my awareness. I stood up at one point and began to feel the actual physical sensation of being born - my body bracing, flinching, wincing, and contracting as it was pushed out from a womb and into the open. This all happened too fast to understand or control.

Then, I opened my eyes and looked at my apartment from the opposite side of the room, staring back toward the futon where I had been previously sitting. There was a poster I had made and put on the wall above the futon, which my eyes became fixated on. It was a simple affirmation that read: ALL IS FULL OF LOVE.

I walked up to it, my eyes wide open in awe, and stared - letting the monumental truth of these words move through me. Suddenly, from this angle, the life I had created for myself didn't look too bad. It looked like I had surrounded myself with beauty and reminders that love is a fundamental virtue.

"Things look completely different from a different angle," the inner voice said, almost mocking me.

For the next several hours, I walked around my tiny apartment and talked out loud. I spent time touching my houseplants and feeling their ecstatic energy send warm shivers through me. I stared at the book I wrote and felt my shame around it dissolve as another consciousness explained its beauty to me.

And then, I received something that I can only describe as instructions: A voice told me that I was becoming ill from not being intimate with a woman for so long. It said that I am not complete on my own - that I am fundamentally incomplete as a man - that I require intimacy with another to receive a kind of balance or spiritual nourishment. I had become starved of this and withered.

According to this voice, I had to be with a woman to find this balance. It wasn't something I could do on my own, and it wasn't something I could find without the vulnerability of intimacy. It wanted me to have sex. There was a sense of urgency to this voice, and although its advice was something I might have eagerly embraced in my horny youth, at this moment, it made me feel sick.

"You have to do this," it declared. *"Your fear of rejection is the only reason you're robbing yourself of this beauty in life. Your fear of feelings - of being hurt or hurting someone else. You can't hide from this intimacy any longer. It will make you sick - It's making you sick."*

Throughout this entire experience, I'd suffered from a pain in my hips that had bothered me intermittently over the previous several months. I attributed this pain to periods of excessive sitting or not stretching enough. But at this moment, the mushrooms had another analysis: *"The pain in your hips is there because that part of your body is essentially rusting,"* the voice said. *"Your sexuality is locked up, frozen, rusted shut. The pain goes away when you open yourself and are touched."*

I was pretty sure stretching helped too, but the point was noted.

For quite some time, this dialogue or guidance continued. I was repeatedly shown how I had withered inside without physical intimacy. And I felt how uncomfortable the idea of putting myself out into the world and looking for love or sex made me.

I had become incredibly comfortable and happy alone. At least, that's what I thought. I had been able to focus on things like writing books and experiencing love in many other ways. But there was an undeniable terror at the vulnerability of sex and intimacy with a woman. Perhaps this was why I was being pushed toward it - it would help me become stronger and force me out of my comfortable hiding.

Before the mushrooms began to fade and I collapsed in exhaustion, there was another interesting side note to this message: The voice told me that writing was one of the only other ways I could balance this incomplete part of myself. Whatever nourishment came from romantic love and sex also came from entering the creative state. In both of these acts, there was an element of touching the divine, interacting with the womb of creation, and being in an intimate relationship with something greater than myself - being in direct contact with a mystery so beautiful it is beyond comprehension.

Still, the voice had an urgency compelling me to find a mate: *"Start your search right now,"* it screamed in my head. *"Don't put this off - you must do this as soon as possible!"*

As the mushroom trip ended, that sense of urgency left an impression on me - I knew I had some things to do. I also knew I wouldn't be taking mushrooms again for a while. It felt like I'd just had my ass kicked, and I came out of that experience knowing it wouldn't be necessary to go back for more any time soon.

Over the following weeks, I reorganized and redecorated my apartment. I also started a more rigorous practice of writing every day. I knew I needed to start dating, too, but I had gotten so used to being alone that it was going to be painful and awkward to break that habit and meet new people. Still, I could feel an urgency stirring in me, pushing me toward my fear.

As I grappled with this, I felt an extraordinary sense of how incomplete I was. In the most liberating way, I had an overwhelming awareness that there was something fundamentally empty in me - a place I could never fill up or make whole on my own. It could only be made whole through the environment, connection, and life. Feeling sickened and nervous at the new challenge in front of me, I realized that this sense of emptiness might never end. But it might be the most beautiful thing.

Dedication

This book is dedicated to my parents, Ken and Lynda Olsen. Thank you for giving me the gift of this life and showing me the love and support that has made everything in it possible. My love and gratitude for both of you is beyond words.

From the author

To anyone who has read this far, thank you for welcoming this book into your world. I hope you have enjoyed the stories contained in these pages - and if you have, please consider giving this book a review on Amazon (or any other online marketplace/platform). This is incredibly helpful in spreading the book's message and will also make me extremely grateful.

If you want to see what I am up to and sharing with the world, visit *milesolsen.com*, where you can also join my newsletter.

Made in United States
Troutdale, OR
02/19/2024

17812942R10116